Chased by Sea Monsters

Prehistoric
predators
of the deep

Chased
by Sea
Monsters

Prehistoric
predators
of the deep

Nigel Marven

Jasper James

For my son Theo
NIGEL MARVEN

For my funny little family
JASPER JAMES

This book is published to accompany the television series entitled *Chased by Sea Monsters*, which was produced by Impossible Pictures and first broadcast on Discovery in 2004.

Series producer and director: Jasper James
Executive producer: Tim Haines
Executive producer for the BBC: Adam Kemp

First American edition, 2004
01 02 03 04 05 10 9 8 7 6 5 4 3 2 1

Published in the United States by DK Publishing, Inc.
375 Hudson Street
New York, New York 10014

Library of Congress Cataloging in Publication data is available for this book.
ISBN 0-7566-0357-7

Commissioning Editors: Shirley Patton and Nicky Ross
Project Editor: Sarah Miles
Copy Editor: Caroline Taggart
Art Director: Linda Blakemore
Designer: Martin Hendry
Line Illustrator: Alan Burton
Picture Researchers: Miriam Hyman and Claire Parker
Production Controller: Arlene Alexander

Set in Janson and Franklin Gothic
Printed and bound in Great Britain by Butler & Tanner Ltd., Frome
Color separations by Radstock Reproductions Ltd, Midsomer Norton

All imperial equivalents are approximate and no equivalent for metric tonnes has been given. One short ton (US) is equivalent to 0.907 metric tonnes.

Page 1: Nigel rides on the back of an archelon, a giant turtle from the Cretaceous.
Page 2: A giant mosasaur leaps out of the water to grab a passing pteranodon.

See our complete product line at www.dk.com

Contents

Nigel flees from a tarbosaurus on a visit to Mongolia, 75 million years ago, for *The Giant Claw: A Walking with Dinosaurs Special.*

Foreword

I have always found animals enthralling. An old cine film of me when I'm less than a year old shows my face crinkling into a smile as a seagull flies over my carriage. I spent my childhood scouring the ponds and meadows near my Hertfordshire home for amphibians and reptiles. It was always thrilling to find a great crested newt in the bottom of my net; at 15 centimeters (6 inches) long these are the biggest amphibians in Britain. My breath would catch if I saw a grass snake gliding across a pond. The largest reptile in Britain, they average 1 meter (3 feet) in length, but record breakers have exceeded 2 meters (6 feet).

My parents thought I'd grow out of my passion, but I made animals my career. Creating wildlife films has taken me all the way to the tropics, where I have encountered the largest reptiles alive today. In Indonesia I met komodo dragons, lizards that can exceed 3 meters (10 feet) in length, and in the swamps of Venezuela I grappled with anacondas, massive snakes that are reputed to grow over 6 meters (20 feet) long. Finding these creatures has always been exhilarating, but occasionally I'd daydream about traveling back in time to when creatures with scales ruled the planet – the age of reptiles.

I thought that was only a fantasy, but that was before I met the team behind *Walking with Dinosaurs*. My first mission with them, for *The Giant Claw*, was to travel back 75 million years to find therizinosaurus, the owner of a giant claw some 71 centimeters (28 inches) long; on the way I was chased by a tarbosaurus, the Asian relative of tyrannosaurus rex. In a second adventure, *Land of Giants*, I paid a visit to Argentina, 100 million years ago, and watched a pack of gigantosaurus, even larger than tyrannosaurus rex, hunt down argentinosaurus, a dinosaur nearly 30 meters (100 feet) long. These were thrilling adventures that I never dared hope to experience. But once you get the bug for time travel it's difficult to stop, and I wanted more.

My other great passion is sharks. I've swum with most of the biggest alive today, but prehistoric sharks were huge and extraordinary as well, so coauthor Jasper James (also the producer and director of the *Sea Monsters* series) came up with a mouthwatering prospect – I would travel back in time to come face to face with long extinct sharks and marine reptiles, sometimes even on the same dive. I'd be immersed in the seven deadliest seas of all time, voyaging through millions of years of evolutionary history to dive with megalodon, the biggest flesh-eating shark ever, and tanystropheus, a peculiar marine reptile with a neck like a giraffe's.

Each phase in prehistory had its own spectacular sea creatures and I was excited about seeing them all. I longed to see the terrifying dunkleosteus, who was king of the oceans when fish were the only backboned creatures around – an armored fish some 10 meters (33 feet) long with serrated plates of bone in its mouth for slicing through its prey. I wanted to meet sea scorpions as well – with their raptorial front legs bristling with spines and spikes for shredding prey, these hunters menaced the sea floor in Ordovician times. Liopleurodon, arguably the biggest predator ever to have lived (up to 25 meters/80 feet in length), would send a shiver down anyone's spine, but using a sort of force field of smell for protection, I'd be able to dive with them.

Which of the seven seas was the deadliest is a matter of opinion. We've made our own choice, and I wonder if you'll agree. Would you rather face off a megalodon, a giant orthocone or a mosasaur? Read this book and watch the series to make up your own mind.

Nigel Marven

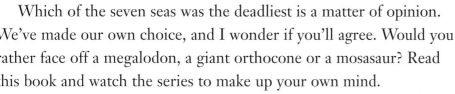

Nigel surfaces from a dive that brought him face to face with the huge flesh-eating shark megalodon. It's no wonder he looks a little shaken.

Introduction

There is something deep in the human psyche which links the ocean with fear. It is fortunate, then, that we evolved only a few hundred thousand years ago; otherwise we would have spent most of prehistory scared out of our wits. The kind of creatures that make us think twice about swimming these days – the great white sharks, the box jellyfish, the sea snakes – are all fairly pathetic compared to what the Earth has seen during the mind-boggling period of time since life began. If you were to travel back to the oceans of prehistory, you would find staggering monsters every bit as terrible as anything science fiction has ever conjured up. The aim of this book is to help you to do just that. We want to take you on a nightmarish safari, to dive deep into the past and visit the seven deadliest seas of all time.

The seven different time zones we will visit range from half a billion to just a few million years ago. The specific times have been chosen because they are the worst of the worst, home to the most horrendous predators the sea has ever known. Each of the following chapters will allow you to get up close and personal with them, but before you do, this introduction will afford you a glimpse of the bigger picture: the ebb and flow of evolution that gave rise to such uniquely monstrous marine life and the circumstances that conspired to wipe it out. In short, in just a few pages, we're going to try to romp through the epic story of life in the ocean – hold on tight!

The story starts long before life had made any impact whatsoever on land. In fact there has been life in the sea for over 3.5 billion years – that's a good seven times longer than it has existed on land. Let's begin even further back, 4 billion years ago, on an Earth

The giants of the Triassic ocean were the ichthyosaurs – of all the marine reptiles, these were the best adapted to life in the sea, with flippers instead of legs and a streamlined body shape similar to that of a dolphin.

In its early days, the Earth was one hell of a planet. In fact for most of its 4-billion-year history, conditions on Earth have been so inhospitable that humans wouldn't have been able to survive.

peppered with volcanoes, where each eruption was not just ash and lava, but also huge quantities of water vapour that condensed in the skies to cause massive, non-stop rainstorms. The Earth was lit up with thunderstorms that raged over slowly forming pools in the blackened rock. Bigger pools swallowed smaller pools to form lakes that grew with relentless slowness into mighty bodies of water – and Earth had its very first oceans.

Back then, the Earth was as wild a planet as you could imagine. If a group of humans were to go back there, they'd be unlikely to survive for much more than a minute. But it wouldn't be the ferociously high levels of UV radiation that would kill them, nor the continual pounding from asteroids and comets, nor even the hugely acidic rain – it would be suffocation. Today the atmosphere is 20 per cent oxygen; 4 billion years ago it was less than 1 per cent. It was the absence of this one vital ingredient – without which neither animals nor plants can breathe – that prevented life really taking off in the oceans for another 2 billion years. Only then would there be enough oxygen to allow anything but the most specialized of life forms to evolve.

The biological big bang

That, then, was our world 4 billion years ago. An angry place seemingly totally unsuitable for life, but under these conditions life did begin – very, very slowly. Some 3.5 billion years ago the first single-celled organisms appeared and then, over a long-drawn-out, 3-billion-year period, the first multi-cellular ones, eventually the first animals, and then *bang*! – life took off. The Cambrian period (half a billion years ago) saw the sudden arrival of all the major animal groups: the arthropods, cephalopods, corals, jellyfish, molluscs, vertebrates, echinoderms. So remarkable is the proliferation of new fossils in the rocks from this time that palaeontologists have dubbed it 'the Cambrian Explosion'. And among all the spectacular new weird and wonderful creatures and body shapes was a rather unspectacular little animal called myllokunmingia. Though only the size of a safety pin, it signalled something of monumental importance: the first fish had arrived.

If you follow your family tree back far enough, you will eventually find a little fish like myllokunmingia. It represents far more than just the beginning of fish-kind – it was also the first animal with a backbone, and from these humble beginnings stems the most adaptable group of life on the planet: the vertebrates. Human beings, dinosaurs, birds, sharks and frogs – basically anything with a backbone – owes its existence to some tiny little fish in the Cambrian.

One theory for the success of the vertebrate design is that it allows the brain and nervous system to be separate from the other organs of the body. The brain is in the head, while the spinal cord is neatly housed inside the backbone. Compare that to an arthropod (such as a lobster) whose 'brain' (for want of a better word) is a ring of tissue around its gut. A bigger brain can't evolve in arthropods because the tissue would squeeze the gut. This hasn't stopped them being incredibly successful, but it has limited their intellect a little. Vertebrates meanwhile have had the freedom to experiment with bigger brains, opening up a world of larger bodies, more sophisticated senses, more complex movement and, ultimately, more success at chess.

Stromatolites – one of the first signs of life. These column-like structures are built up by colonies of photosynthesizing algae and first appear in the fossil record 3.5 billion years ago. They are still around today – these ones are from Shark Bay in Western Australia.

The first monsters

Over the last 370 million years the world's biggest predators have all been vertebrates, descended from some little fish in the Cambrian. But members of the fish-lineage certainly didn't have it all their own way to start with. They had to endure a period further down the food chain at the mercy of various oversized creepy-crawlies. Chapter 1 takes a close look at the first of the deadly seas, 450 million years ago – so long ago that life had not even arrived on land – in a period called the Ordovician. The world then was a truly inhospitable place. It was in the Ordovician that the first giant

The life and times of planet Earth

ORDOVICIAN
Chapter 1

DEVONIAN
Chapter 2

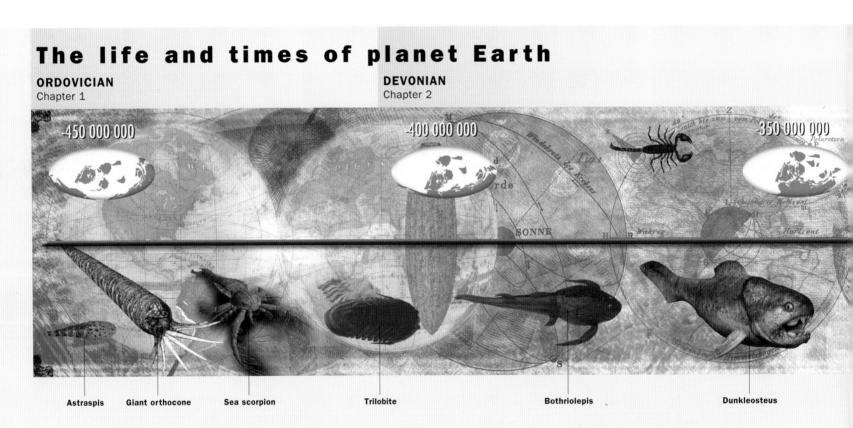

-450 000 000

-400 000 000

-350 000 000

Astraspis   Giant orthocone   Sea scorpion   Trilobite   Bothriolepis   Dunkleosteus

The Ordovician saw the first truly enormous predator on earth – the giant orthocone, which measured up to 12 metres (40 feet) long.

Trilobites were a hugely successful group, which came in all shapes and sizes and were an ever-present feature of the seas for 300 million years, until they became extinct 250 million years ago.

The Devonian is known as the 'Age of Fishes'. The meanest of all of them were the placoderms – a group of fish with armoured heads.

predators emerged, and worst among them were the massive tentacled orthocones. These really were the original sea monsters, but they weren't the only creatures around that looked like escapees from a horror story: the shallower waters were teeming with sea scorpions – vicious, hideous, oversized, twin-clawed relatives of spiders and land scorpions. Some species, such as pterogotus, grew to more than 2 metres (7 feet) in length. The scorpions eventually took over as top predators when the orthocones relinquished their stranglehold on life; the giant forms disappeared some 417 million years ago.

For 300 million years trilobites were as common as muck in the seas of prehistory. Most species lived on the seabed and fed on organic sediment.

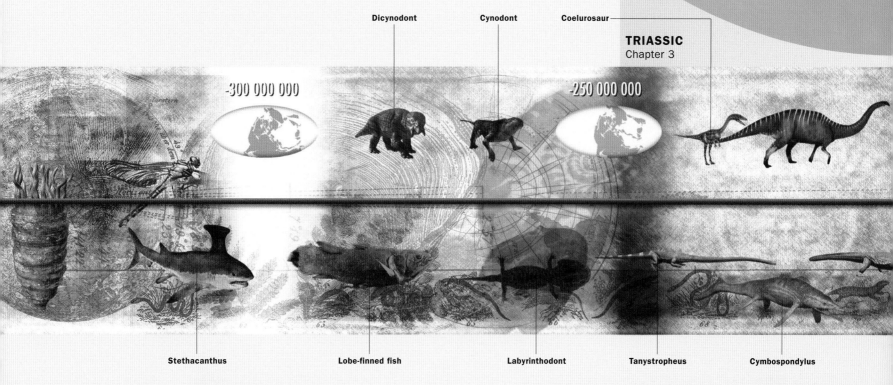

Dicynodont Cynodont Coelurosaur

TRIASSIC
Chapter 3

-300 000 000

-250 000 000

Stethacanthus Lobe-finned fish Labyrinthodont Tanystropheus Cymbospondylus

The first sharks appeared in the Devonian and took over as top predators in the Carboniferous period.

By the early Triassic reptiles had not only adapted to life in the ocean, they had also become the largest animals there.

13

Age of fishes

Meanwhile the fish had started to toughen up. To make themselves harder targets for the sea scorpions' claws, they developed body armour. The Ordovician fish astraspis looked like a reinforced tadpole with the whole head and body region encased in a box of thick bone, its mouth little more than an opening in the front. It had no fins and only the tail retained any flexibility. Not the most manoeuvrable of arrangements, but this was a fish that spent its life sucking in detritus from the seafloor – it didn't need speed to do that, but it did need protection while doing it. All in all, the strategy

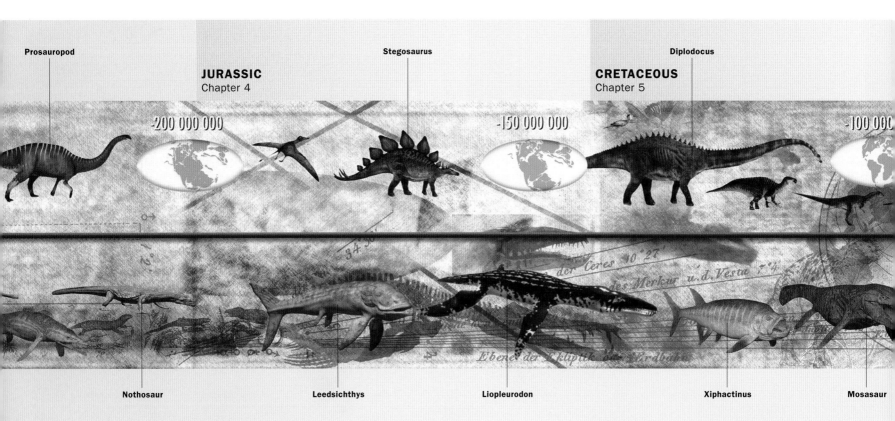

Prosauropod

JURASSIC
Chapter 4

Stegosaurus

-200 000 000

-150 000 000

Diplodocus

CRETACEOUS
Chapter 5

-100 000

Nothosaur

Leedsichthys

Liopleurodon

Xiphactinus

Mosasaur

In the Jurassic animals became truly enormous – not only on land with the dinosaurs, but also in the water with the gargantuan fish *Leedsichthys* and the collosal *Liopleurodon*, a marine reptile that could have been the largest predator of all time.

The end of the Cretaceous is most famous for *Tyrannosaurus rex*, but in fact the ocean had a whole host of predators of its own to brag about – the grotesque fish *Xiphactinus* and the awesome mosasaurs, a group of marine reptiles related to snakes but a whole lot bigger.

must have worked, because subsequent fish stuck with it, experimenting with a variety of different forms of armour.

By 360 million years ago, the start of the Devonian period, the seas were teeming with fish called placoderms ('plated skin'). These still had the body protection of their predecessors, but married it with a vital new feature – jaws. With jaws, fish were liberated from the filter-feeding lifestyle of their earlier relatives. They could start eating other animals, and they did.

Enter the star of Chapter 2, dunkleosteus. This placoderm was built for speed – it still had armour, but only on its head. Moreover, at over 9 metres (30 feet) long, dunkleosteus rocked the sea world and put the fish firmly at the top of the food chain.

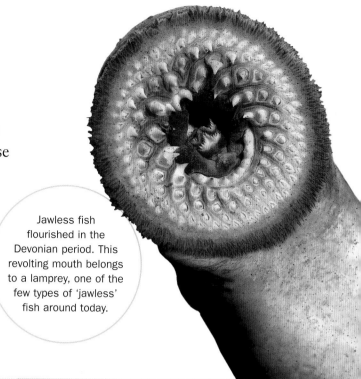

Jawless fish flourished in the Devonian period. This revolting mouth belongs to a lamprey, one of the few types of 'jawless' fish around today.

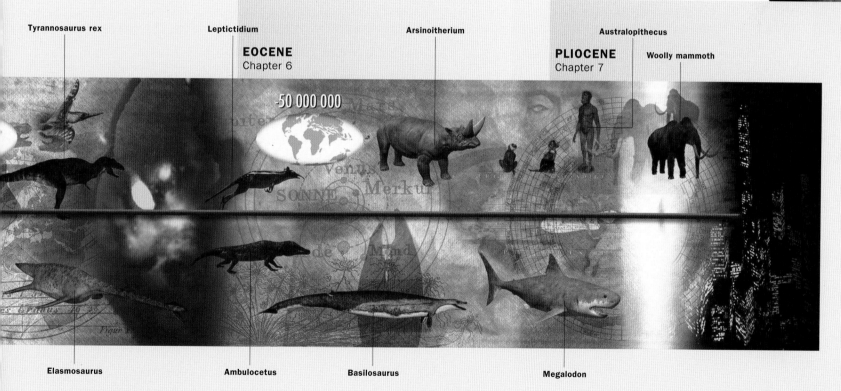

Tyrannosaurus rex

Leptictidium

Arsinoitherium

EOCENE
Chapter 6

-50 000 000

Australopithecus

PLIOCENE
Chapter 7

Woolly mammoth

Elasmosaurus

Ambulocetus

Basilosaurus

Megalodon

When dinosaurs became extinct, marine reptiles were also wiped out.

Whales evolved from land animals and became enormous towards the end of the Eocene.

At about the same time as our ancestors first walked upright, the ocean was home to the monstrous *Megalodon*, a shark so large that it preyed on whales.

15

A small reminder of the first fish to set fin on land. Mudskippers can spend periods of time out of the water and even climb the mangrove trees among which they live.

While dunkleosteus was busy chomping its way through anything it wanted, other types of fish were appearing in the background: fish that had the jaws, but not the armour. And so arrived a more familiar breed of marine monster, and some of the most accomplished killers of all time – the sharks.

Meanwhile, some very odd things were happening out of the water. The land was no longer the barren waste it had been in the Ordovician, but had been colonized by weird-looking plants, including the first trees. Animals were also moving in to this new frontier. On the shores of estuaries and lakes some pioneering fish had come out of the water and were flopping about between shallow pools by pulling themselves along on their flippers. And if that isn't a weird enough thought, one of them (rhizodus) was almost 8.5 metres (28 feet) long, and had tusks – yes, tusks. There is evidence to suggest that some of these 'landfish' waited on the top of steep riverbanks in order to ambush fish in the water below by sliding down the mud.

These were the first inelegant steps toward life on land. Next would be the evolution of the amphibians – animals that can breathe air but must return to the water to breed.

Things were almost as strange in the sea: the first sharks, it has to be said, looked completely and utterly absurd. Luckily for them, though, looks aren't everything and with the placoderms dying out, the early sharks such as stethacanthus came to dominate the sea during the Carboniferous, the period which followed the Devonian.

Return to the water

Sharks were to have it all their own way for over 100 million years, but then competition came from a totally unexpected direction: the land. Reptiles were busy taking over air, land and sea. This was the

Nigel gets to grips with a nothosaur. At 4 metres (13 feet 6 inches) long, it's one of the first big sea reptiles.

beginning of one of the most spectacular eras in Earth's history, a period of 170 million years when reptiles had the world sewn up.

So where did these new rulers come from? Well, on the margins between air and water, life had undergone revolutionary change. Fish had given rise to amphibians, and amphibians in turn had given rise to reptiles, which were far less dependent on the water. Then, some 290 million years ago, the planet was hit by a major ice age. Ice ages are actually extremely dry periods, because low temperatures mean less evaporation, which means less rain (the exact opposite of a hot, steamy, rainforest climate). This made life desperately hard for the water-needy amphibians, but the reptiles were more than able to cope and they flourished.

And then came the new twist in the march of evolution – reptiles started moving back into their ancestral home, the sea. By now, of course, they had changed beyond recognition; they were air-breathing animals built for life on land. The first wave of ocean-going reptiles didn't amount to much, but then about 245 million years ago a second wave started dipping their scaly toes in the water.

To begin with, these newcomers couldn't shake their land-based origins. They had to breathe air and continued to return to land to lay their eggs. But what marine reptiles did have was more brain, more body and more brawn. These qualities were enough to give them the upper hand, and within 10 million years they had ousted the fish from the top-predator business. One group, the ichthyosaurs, were so well adapted to the water that they no longer even returned to the beach to lay eggs. Chapter 3 deals with this new collection of marine killers: the toothy nothosaur, the sleek ichthyosaur cymbospondylus and the weirdest animal of all time, tanystropheus.

The Cretaceous killer sarcosuchus was a 12-metre (40-foot) long relative of the crocodile, and preyed on dinosaurs of all shapes and sizes.

Hell's aquarium

The Cretaceous was the worst time to get in the water, but the land was no picnic either. These are velociraptors – they may not be as huge as other predatory dinosaurs, but they are fast, well armed and hunt in packs.

Round about the time that sea reptiles started to rule the waves, the first dinosaurs were appearing on land. To start with these legendary lords of the land were nothing much to look at. Dinosaurs would, of course, get a lot bigger and nastier as time went by, but what most people don't realize is that, throughout their reign on land, the dinosaurs were consistently outdone in size and nastiness by their reptilian relatives in the sea.

Some Triassic sea reptiles, dating back 220 million years, reached astonishing sizes: shonisaurus was around 15 metres (50 feet) long, but ate mainly squid. Another newly discovered ichthyosaur measured 25 metres (80 feet) long. But these early giants were gentle ones. By contrast the marine reptiles in the Jurassic (about 50 million years ago) were well worth having nightmares about: at over 20 metres (65 feet), the monstrously lethal liopleurodon is definitely a contender for the title of scariest sea creature of all time. And things got even worse by the end of the Cretaceous, the last great period of reptile dominance. In addition to reptiles like the giant mosasaur (the other main candidate for scariest sea creature ever), there were a whole host of oversized killers in the water, including a 6-metre (20-foot) long fish called xiphactinus that could probably have swallowed a cow whole – if only cows had evolved by then.

Let's pause for a minute and take stock of what the world was like 75 million years ago. It was, in a word, terrifying. In no period of its history has the planet seen such an awesome collection of killers as at the end of the Cretaceous. The water teamed with nightmarish creatures, and homicidal monsters, such as tyrannosaurus rex and the raptors, ruled the land. If time-travel tourism ever becomes a reality, expect very high insurance premiums for visiting the Cretaceous.

End of an era

At the beginning of the Eocene period it looked as though birds had taken the place of dinosaurs – gastornis was almost 2 metres (6 feet) tall and the top predator of its time.

But all this scariness was about to be turned on its head in the most high-profile extinction event of them all: 65 million years ago – the time when the dinosaurs took their final curtain. A planet poisoned by raging volcanic activity, deeply disturbed climatic patterns, a 10-kilometre (6-mile) wide comet plunging into the gulf of Mexico – these are the factors that contributed to the demise of dinosaur-kind. And what about all the sea monsters: the giant mosasaurs and the other denizens of the deep? Well, they went too, bringing to an end prehistory's worst ever time to get in the water.

The Earth probably doesn't contemplate these things too deeply, but if it did it would have been thinking, 'What a waste of all that evolution, now I've got to start again.' Or alternatively it might have been glad to see the back of so many unpleasant animals, and hoping for something nicer next time. Most likely, though, it just sat and span in space, while on its surface the survivors of the extinction battled it out for world domination.

Sharks obviously made it through – and with all the big marine reptiles gone they suddenly found themselves top of the heap. On land things weren't so cut and dried. Insects, reptiles and mammals all found themselves on an equal footing. For a while the birds took over, and the world became a little like a Lewis Carroll story. Imagine a forest where 2-metre (6-foot) birds wander around, preying on miniature horses. So it was on Earth 50 million years ago. But you wouldn't be sitting reading this if it wasn't for the fact that the eventual winners of the struggle to be the planet's dominant life form were the mammals.

Murderous mammals

Mammals succeeded because they were just so adaptable. They moved into every niche, including the water. And this is where we get back to the story of the ocean. Around the same time that the birds ruled, the mammals were busy repeating the same trick that the reptiles had pulled almost 200 million years earlier. They moved from the land into the water. A creature called ambulocetus was one of the pioneers; looking for all the world like an oversized otter, this 2.5-metre (8-foot) fur-ball lived like a crocodile, hiding just under the surface of the water and grabbing anything unfortunate enough to wander by. Ambulocetus was more than just a curiosity – it was the beginning of the most magnificent dynasty of ocean-dwellers, the whales.

A group of dorudon mob a basilosaurus that is threatening their newborn calves. Both prey and predator are types of primitive whale that thrived 36 million years ago in the Tethys Sea, an ancient waterway running between Asia and Africa.

Early whales had to stay close to river mouths and sources of fresh water because their kidneys were unable to deal with salt water. This constraint kept them to a modest size. Only later, when they had evolved the ability to process sea water, could whales really start to colonize the deep blue oceans away from shore, and grow to leviathan proportions. By 40 million years ago, they had taken over from the sharks – not just in size, but also in meanness. These were very different whales from the ones we're used to. Nowadays they're generally big, blubbery and gentle, more gum than tooth. But back then they were sleek, ferocious giants, packing the kind of dentition that wouldn't have looked out of place on a dinosaur. Basilosaurus was undoubtedly the worst of the bunch – not only did it eat sharks, it ate other whales as well.

Basilosaurus died out 36 million years ago and it wasn't until 20 million years later that the sharks got their own back – in spectacular fashion. The last chapter of this book is dedicated to a fish that beggars belief: megalodon, the mega-tooth shark. Some 15 metres (50 feet) long and, at 48 tonnes, the weight of over 20 great white sharks, this monster of the deep kept hunger at bay by biting whales in half. Fortunately, megalodon died out 1.6 million years ago – so the only way to see one these days is to have a thoroughly bad nightmare.

So that's the big picture. Seven deadly seas that no one in their right mind would want to go swimming in. But now it's time to put your (quite rational) fears to one side because, deadly or not, we're about to plunge right in …

The seven
most deadly seas
of all time

Rating	Period	Date
1st	Cretaceous	75 million years ago
2nd	Jurassic	155 million years ago
3rd	Pliocene	4 million years ago
4th	Eocene	36 million years ago
5th	Devonian	360 million years ago
6th	Triassic	230 million years ago
7th	Ordovician	450 million years ago

450

million years ago

The Ordovician

The predators from half a billion years ago are, fortunately, unlike anything in the twenty-first century. Tentacled orthocones measuring 11 metres (36 feet) long and the ever-present sea scorpions make this alien world a nightmarish one.

No place for humans

Any human visiting the Ordovician is in for a shock. It is an assault on your breathing, your sight, your smell and even your mind. And that's just the land ... to get in the water here is to experience a habitat so alien that you'll have a hard time believing you are still on Earth.

Step out on to any part of the planet during the Ordovician, and the first thing you notice is that you might as well be on the moon – the Earth is completely barren. You are so far back in time that life has yet to colonize the land. The closest examination of the ground reveals hardly more than a single speck of life – at most a stain of lichen or liverwort under a rock. Aside from that there are no plants, no animals, no nothing. The silence is absolutely deafening.

As you move towards the coast you find yourself straining for breath. You push on, but soon the breathlessness moves to nausea

Lichen was one of the only signs of life on land at this time. It is an alliance between two of the earliest life forms – algae and fungi – which live together as one organism. The alga converts the sunlight to sugar for food, while the fungus provides the outer structure.

We might think of coral reefs as part and parcel of ocean life, but they didn't even exist before the Ordovician.

YOU ARE HERE

The Ordovician at a glance

How bad? Seventh most dangerous sea (nickname – the Ordovicious).
How long ago? 450 million years.
Where? New York (or what will become New York). Giant species of orthocone can also be found in what will become northern Europe.
Shape of the continents: You'd be hard pressed to recognize Earth from the Ordovician world map – the position of the continents is completely different from the familiar layout of today. Gondwana, made up of what will one day become Africa, South America, Australia and Antarctica, is the biggest continent by far and straddles the southern hemisphere. The next biggest landmass is Laurentia, situated on the Equator and made up of bits of Europe and North America.
What's new? The first coral reefs appear during the Ordovician.

THE HAZARDS
Top predator: *Orthocone.*
Other predators: *Eurypterids* (or sea scorpions).
Atmosphere: The air has only 15 per cent oxygen, compared with 20 per cent in the twenty-first century. This, though, is less of a problem than the higher levels of CO_2 – 0.5 per cent, as opposed to 0.03 per cent today. Side effects of breathing high CO_2 include hyperventilation, nausea and headaches.
Day length: Because the Earth spins just over 10 per cent faster in the Ordovician than today, the day is a mere 21 hours long. The human body-clock expects a day length of around 24 hours. So the Ordovician 21-hour days would play the same kind of havoc with a person's body-clock as jet lag does. In fact, over the course of several days, it would be considerably worse. Since every day is three hours too short, the body would never be able to adjust – it would be like flying three time zones to the east every day. Longer-term visitors would be even more confused, with months being 35 days and years 417 days long.
On shore: Nothing to worry about, apart from sunstroke.

Hell
on earth

Given that there has been life in the water for some 3 billion years by now, it seems unbelievable that barely a single foot or frond has found its way on to the land. The truth is (and this will seem strange to us landlubbing humans) that the open air is a far more hostile environment than the underwater world.

Living on land presents an organism with a whole number of challenges that just don't apply to living in the sea. For a start, it places hefty demands on the body – it has to support its own weight. Not so for marine animals. Take the jellyfish – it can virtually ignore gravity because it is naturally buoyant in salt water. Getting by on land requires a weight-bearing structure, which is why jellyfish never get far up the beach. And in animals that structure needs to be designed not just for staying upright but also for moving along the ground in search of food and resources, something that requires a far more sophisticated set-up than swimming does. Second, to live in air an organism needs a way of retaining its water, so that it isn't lost too quickly to evaporation. (By contrast, dehydration is not something ocean life forms have to worry about.) Lastly, sea water is rich in food and nutrients, which means that some ocean plants and animals can get all they need from the water around them. This is a luxury not available on land. These problems weren't really overcome until the Devonian period (see Chapter 2).

and finally a splitting headache kicks in. You are starting to experience the side effects of visiting a world before plants. Plants convert carbon dioxide (CO_2) to oxygen and without them the atmosphere is completely different from what humans are used to. There is a quarter less oxygen and almost twice as much CO_2. It is the increased levels of CO_2 that give the biggest problem – the urge to breathe is caused by the amount of CO_2 in your lungs. In these high levels your body is perpetually fighting to bring in more air, but with every lungful comes more CO_2 – it is an uncomfortable vicious circle. To survive here for long you need to bring your own air.

Because of the lack of plants, the atmosphere is completely different from what humans are used to, with far less oxygen and more carbon dioxide. So, if you're visiting the Ordovician, make sure you take your own air!

You are approaching New York, or what will be New York in half a billion years' time. In the Ordovician it is the coastline of the huge island of Laurentia. You can see in the distance where the desert gives way to the ocean. If the atmosphere hasn't already made you nauseous, what you're about to experience certainly will. As you move closer to the sea, your nostrils start bearing the full onslaught of another Ordovician nastiness – a stench so loathsome that you can hardly stop your stomach from turning itself inside out. Holding your nose, you struggle on to the beach to see piles of gunk oozing out of the washed-up carcasses of ten of thousands of rotting sea creatures: armoured fish, sea urchins, horseshoe crabs, trilobites, nautiloids, corals – all manner of death coughed up by the sea. In the future, there will be scavengers around on land to pick the beach clean, but here in the Ordovician the mounting pile of oceanic phlegm goes untouched, left to decompose under the sun.

As you survey this fetid scene, the sun starts to set. Just 3 p.m., says your watch, but you might as well throw it away. Days in the

Horse-shoe crabs and dead fish lie rotting on an Ordovician beach. In later times there will be scavengers to pick the beach clean.

Ordovician are a mere 21 hours long. This strange quirk of time occurs because day length is a direct result of the speed of the Earth's rotation, and since our planet first formed it has been slowing down. Over the half-billion years between the Ordovician and the twenty-first century it will slow enough to add three hours to the time it takes to do one revolution. The human body-clock expects a day length of about 24 hours – so if you stay in the place for more than a day you'll start to experience constant, inescapable and ever-worsening jet lag.

And you aren't even in the water yet …

Nasty nippers

Though nothing lives on land, the odd set of footprints can be seen on the wet sand just out of the water. In some ways they are like the tracks of an insect, with two parallel lines made by the creature's feet. But the distance between the feet reveals that this is bigger than any insect. However, the tracks extend no further than a metre or two inland and then lead straight back into the water. It is easy to miss their importance: these are more than just footprints in the sand; they are evidence of a landmark event in the Earth's history. The owners of these tracks are among the first life forms to walk on the ground. For life this is an achievement every bit as phenomenal as landing on the moon. Yet these creatures are no more at home on land than Neil Armstrong was on the lunar surface and, after their brief beach forays, they turn back to the sea where they belong.

To follow their tracks into the water is to be hit by a wave of contrast. Above the water is a dead calm of nothingness, while under it rages a storm of extraordinary life – finless fish with armoured

Trilobites

One of the first recorded finds of a trilobite fossil was by a Dr Lhwyd in 1698 – he wrote in a letter to an acquaintance that he had found the skeleton of 'some flatfish'. 'Flat' maybe, but 'fish' was way off the mark. What he should have written was that he'd found the exoskeleton of an ancient arthropod and one of considerable importance. It was the beginning of a palaeontological love affair with the trilobite.

From a human perspective, arthropods are inside-out animals. The soft bits are on the inside, the hard bits such as the joints are on the outside and are called the exoskeleton. Insects, crabs, lobsters are all arthropods, as were the sea scorpions. But of all the early arthropods trilobites were by far the most successful.

The name trilobite means 'three lobes' and if ever an animal deserved the name

This beautifully preserved fossil from the Wolchow river in Russia is of a 12.5-centimetre (5-inch) long trilobite called *Ceraurinella ingrica*.

it was this one: not only was the body split into three lobes lengthways – cephalon, thorax and phygidium (science-speak for head, middle and tail) – but it was also split into three lobes crossways. Essentially it was a shield on legs: the limbs, antennae and vulnerable parts were all on the underside, protected by the hard carapace on top. But unlike the shell of a crab, which is one solid structure, a trilobite's shell was further divided into overlapping segments (as many as 40), which gave the whole animal amazing flexibility. Many species could even roll up into a ball to protect themselves.

Like many trilobites, the extraordinary *Asaphus kowalewskii* would have lived and fed on the sea floor, where its eyes on stalks would have protuded up out of the sediment.

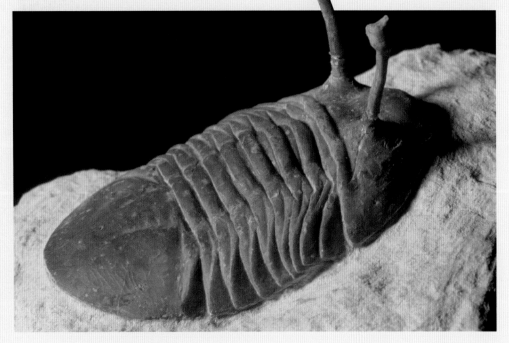

But while all trilobites were built on this basic body plan, they were also all strikingly different. Over the course of the 300 million years they spent trundling across the seabed, there were well over 15,000 species. In fact, they were the single most diverse group of organisms that are now extinct.

From minuscule (under a millimetre/ ⅒₅ inch) to massive (almost 1 metre/ 3 feet); from spiky to smooth; diggers, swimmers, crawlers and floaters; trilobites with small eyes, whopping eyes, no eyes; predators, detritus-eaters, filter-feeders – trilobites came in every flavour.

Given their diversity, it's not surprising that their lifestyles differed. Smaller ones spent their days burrowing into the sediment, munching through bits of dead organic matter. Others swum or floated in mid-water, filtering out micro-organisms. But by and large, trilobites were crawling creatures that hung around the seafloor, waiting for dead or small things to float by. The rather unflattering term for animals with this way of life is 'bottom feeders'.

The single most extraordinary thing about trilobites was their sight, unique in the animal kingdom – they had solid crystalline eyes. Every other animal you can think of has soft eyes, but in the trilobite the eyes were made of lots of small, transparent crystals of calcite which functioned as lenses. The number of lenses in each eye varied between one and as many as 15,000. And correspondingly, there seems to have been every possibility catered for in the shape of the eyes – lenses arranged in dots or crescents,

Some trilobites could roll themselves into a ball for defence against predators – their hard shell was left exposed, while their softer underside was protected.

compound eyes like a fly's, eyes that looked sideways, eyes that looked upwards, huge hemispherical eyes that looked every which way.

All arthropods pay a price for having a shell – it restricts their growth, and in order to grow bigger they have to moult their old shell before secreting a new one. This is another feature that endears trilobites to palaeontologists, since a

single animal could moult ten or even 30 times in its lifetime, leaving cast-offs which have fossilized very well. Trilobite shells leave a remarkably detailed record of their time on Earth: a feast of fossils that charts their amazing 300 million years of success and their complete disappearance at the end of the Permian, 250 million years ago, in the most severe extinction of all.

Astraspis

Astraspis was a small and very primitive fish that had no jaws and no fins. It lived by sifting the seabed for small particles of food and protected itself with a heavy and inflexible head shield. *Astraspis* was probably preyed upon by many other animals, including the sea scorpions and orthocones.

Name: Means 'star shield'.

Type of animal: A primitive jawless fish (agnathan) and a distant relative of the living lamprey and hagfish.

When was it alive? 460–440 million years ago (Mid to Late Ordovician).

Pronunciation: AS-tr-as-pis.

Size: 30 centimetres (12 inches) in length.

Diet: Detritus and small invertebrates found on the seabed.

Fossil finds: North America.

Fact: The only surviving relative of *Astraspis* is the eel-like lamprey fish. In 1135 King Henry I of England died after eating too many lampreys at a banquet!

heads called astraspis, trilobites of every size looking for all the world like gargantuan woodlice, the long, curved shells of small nautiloids moving in pulses past fantastically shaped sponges. And among it all are the owners of the footprints on the beach, animals of fascinating hideousness – the sea scorpions.

The proper name for these creatures is eurypterids, but their appearance is amazingly scorpion-like. They have eight limbs, massive pincers at the front and a tail that can curve up and over. The similarity is no accident – eurypterids are indeed related to scorpions, sharing a common ancestor, but it has to be said that eurypterids are infinitely nastier. The commonest, and without doubt the most intimidating, species of sea scorpion here is

Sea scorpions are one of the few creatures in the Ordovician capable of breathing air. Their gills are adapted to absorb oxygen from both water and the atmosphere.

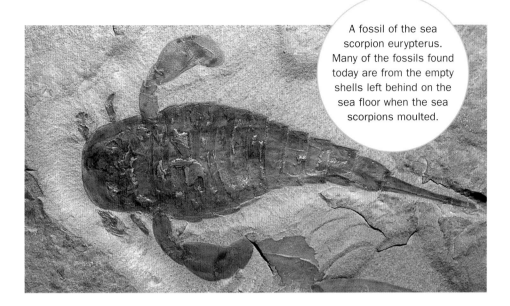

A fossil of the sea scorpion eurypterus. Many of the fossils found today are from the empty shells left behind on the sea floor when the sea scorpions moulted.

Sea scorpions

Resembling giant scorpions and just as deadly, the sea scorpions were the terror of the Ordovician seabed. Also called eurypterids (pronounced YOU-ree-ip-TER-id), the sea scorpions were the all-terrain vehicles of their day and could walk, swim and even venture on to the land. One of the most impressive species was *Megalograptus,* a voracious hunter using its sharp claws and spines to attack and shred fish and other animals.

Name: *Megalograptus* means 'giant writing', possibly because early fossils were mistaken for other animals called graptolites.

Type of animal: A Chelicerate arthropod, in the same group as horseshoe crabs.

When was it alive? Eurypterids in general

megalograptus. It has front pincers bristling with vicious spines which it uses to tear its prey apart. This in fact is its principal weapon, since it lacks the poisonous barb of land scorpions. Most worryingly of all, some megalograptus are nearly 1 metre (3 feet) long. After seeing one of these, you'll never be scared of land scorpions again.

Though far larger predators ply the deeper waters away from the shore, in the shallow lagoons close to the beach the sea scorpions have it very much their own way, demolishing the other inhabitants in a variety of ways. Megalograptus can be seen using the long spines on its front limbs to sweep through the sand and sediment, feeling for worms, crustaceans and the odd armoured fish that might be busy feeding there. These spines are extremely sensitive to vibrations and a quick flurry of a fish tail under the sand will not go unnoticed.

But the sea scorpions also have the equipment to be effective as open-water hunters. Their sight, while not nearly as sophisticated as that of later predators, gives them a crucial advantage over most of the other creatures around. They have a pair of compound eyes –

480–270 million years ago; *Megalograptus* 460–445 million years.

Pronunciation: MEG-ah-lo-grap-tus.

Size: 8 centimetres–2 metres (3 inches– 6 feet 6 inches) in length; *Megalograptus* 1 metre (3 feet).

Diet: Small animals living on the seabed; fish, trilobites and other eurypterids.

Fossil finds: Sea scorpions are found worldwide, but *Megalograptus* only in North America.

Facts: They would get together in their hundreds in order to mate. And eurypterids were the first creatures to walk on land.

much like those of a fly – which can pick out areas of light and dark, and also detect movement. And in one crucial respect these eyes are more like a human's than a fly's – they are not positioned on either side of its head, but face forward, allowing it to see its prey with both eyes at the same time. This is the prerequisite for perceiving objects in three dimensions – so-called 'stereoscopic vision'. As it swims through the shallows, the sea scorpion visually locks on to its victim, using its sight to judge exactly when it is within striking range of its fearsome pincers. Like a praying mantis, it shoots its spiny death traps out in the blink of an eye – with unerring accuracy the victim is trapped, dismembered and moved piecemeal back into the sea scorpion's mouth.

Sea scorpions congregate in shallow water shortly before mating. It is the beginning of a mass invasion – thousands more will soon arrive.

Sex on the beach

There are times when the beach does become more than a pile of rotting corpses. During an equinox, the tides are far higher and the scorpions exploit this rhythm of the seas to reproduce. The first sign is the sudden movement of thousands of sea scorpions towards the shore – as though governed by one collective mind they swarm into the shallows, choking the lagoons with their writhing bodies. But this staggering synchronicity isn't achieved through some mass communication: it is the full moon that triggers them to head *en masse* for the beach.

At these times the sea scorpions literally show their softer side. For them, mating goes hand in hand with moulting. Just like modern crabs and lobsters, sea scorpions crawl out of their old shells to reveal a softer one beneath. Shedding the old shell is the

Sea scorpions, like this megalograptus, can be found in shallow water, close to shore. Handle with care though – they have fearsome claws to deal with their prey.

Sea scorpions spend the vast majority of their time in the water, but at certain times of year, huge groups of them struggle up the beach to mate.

only way they can grow bigger: their flexible new body takes the opportunity to expand before the soft shell hardens around it. Immediately after moulting, even the tough-as-nails sea scorpions become extremely vulnerable, and so moving into shallow water is partly for protection – they are out of reach of the deep-water predators.

But it has another function. The abnormally high tide around an equinox carries the sea scorpions further up the beach than at any other time of year. There they form twisting, thrashing mating mounds. The males deposit packets of sperm (spermatophores),

This modern-day photograph could easily have been taken in the Ordovician. Horse-shoe crabs also exploit the high tide to mate. Unlike the sea scorpions, though, they are still around 450 million years later. These ones are from Cape May in New Jersey.

which the females pick up using their external sexual organs. Once the mating is over, and the tides drop, the fertilized eggs deposited on the beach remain high and dry and can develop out of reach of the many sea creatures that would otherwise eat them.

And then, as suddenly as they arrived, the adults leave, returning to the gloom of deeper water. Among the wasted eggs and discarded skins they have left behind, though, a few adults remain – adults waiting for an easy meal, cannibalizing freshly hatched baby monsters.

Orthocones – a deep-water menace

The sea scorpions in themselves are a good enough reason to be fearful of getting into the Ordovician sea. But their top-predator status holds good only for the shallows. Head out any deeper and the sea scorpions also have to watch their backs. Just 800 metres (½ mile) from the malodorous shoreline the seabed starts to drop dramatically. A mere 9 metres (30 feet) deep becomes 30 metres (100 feet) becomes 300 metres (1000 feet). This plunging wall marks the boundary around a deeper domain ruled by a predator an order

Giant orthocone

Orthocones were the ancient relatives of squid and octopus. Some, such as *Cameroceras*, grew to an enormous size. They lived inside protective shells with only their tentacles showing.
Name: *Cameroceras* means 'chambered horn'. This is because inside its long, straight shell are many smaller chambers that are used to balance it in the water.
Type of animal: A cephalopod mollusc, in the same general group as squid and octopus.
When was it alive? 470–440 million years ago (Late Ordovician and Early Silurian).
Pronunciation: OR-thoh-cone.
Size: 10–11 metres (33–36 feet) total length (shell is 9–10 metres/ 30–33 feet long).
Diet: Fish, trilobites and large arthropods such as sea scorpions.
Fossil finds: North America.
Fact: In Victorian times, people used to think that fossilized orthocone shells were the horns of unicorns.

of magnitude larger than anything else alive at this time; larger, in fact, than anything the Earth has seen in its first 3 billion years of supporting life.

The closest humankind will ever come to seeing anything like this predator is in the nightmares of seventeenth-century sailors. Many a map from that time is adorned with pictures of boats being dragged under by huge, tentacled denizens of the deep. Those particular sea monsters were no more than the figment of a malnourished sailor's delirious imagination, but the huge, tentacled

This picture dates back to around 1700 and shows a huge kraken (a legendary sea monster) attacking a boat during a storm.

denizens of the deep that are found in New York, 450 million years before the twenty-first century, are certainly not.

The ultimate killers of the Ordovician are the orthocones. They belong to a group of shelled molluscs called the nautiloids (orthocones is strictly speaking shorthand – their proper name is 'orthoconic nautiloids', meaning straight-shelled nautiloids). Without doubt, the orthocones are the most impressive nautiloids by far. Their most distinctive features are their astonishing size and their long, tapering shells, which move horizontally through the water. Inside, the shell is divided into as many as 30 chambers, and in the largest one (at the wider end of the shell) lives the business end of the animal – a powerful, crushing, horny beak in the middle of eight huge tentacles, watched over by a pair of chameleon-like eyes. The tentacles betray a family connection – the orthocones are some of the earliest relatives of squid and octopus.

Among the orthocones that cruise slowly through the water, one is truly gigantic: cameroceras. This is a genus found all over the world, but for some reason in these waters their size is more excessive than anywhere else. On larger individuals the shell alone is 9 metres (30 feet) long, with a further 2.5 metres (8 feet) of head and tentacle on top.

At that size, there is nothing else around that can challenge them, and they have their pick of prey, which they set about killing in an amazingly leisurely fashion; orthocones are not the swiftest of creatures and at first sight it is surprising that they can catch anything. To move up and down in the water column, they have to regulate the amount of gas in the empty chambers of their shell, much like a submarine. It is by no means an instantaneous process. Their speed of movement horizontally is appreciably better. Under the tentacles they have a small, flexible tube called a hyponome which they can point in any direction. Orthocones send squirts of water through this tube, pushing themselves in the opposite

Dos and don'ts of Ordovician diving

The Ordovician has some very specific challenges that make diving hazardous. Because of the atmosphere, using scuba equipment is potentially fatal – the effects of the high levels of CO_2 are accelerated because the air in the tank is under pressure. The likely outcome of diving with a tank of compressed Ordovician air would be unconsciousness, followed by death by drowning. Therefore, to dive here requires making up a special mix of air with a much lower level of CO_2.

And then there are the animals to worry about. The abundance of sea scorpions in the water makes them virtually impossible to avoid. An ordinary wet suit offers little protection from them, but the chain-mail suits that twenty-first-century divers use for swimming with sharks are ideal for preventing injury from the scorpions' viciously sharp pincers.

However, no chain-mail suit is going to stop the crushing tentacles of an orthocone. To survive, a diver should aim to stay at the pointy end of the shell – they are very slow to turn.

direction. This 'jet propulsion' works on exactly the same principle as the jet engine – due to be invented in a mere half-billion years' time. However, it is a far-from-perfect system. For the animal to move head first the hyponome has to be bent back on itself, which makes it less efficient, and so orthocones swim faster backwards than they do forwards – one obvious downside being that they cannot see where they are going. Furthermore, they are the antithesis of manoeuvrability: the ballast in their shell forces them to remain horizontal, and the length of their shell gives them turning problems similar to those experienced by oil tankers.

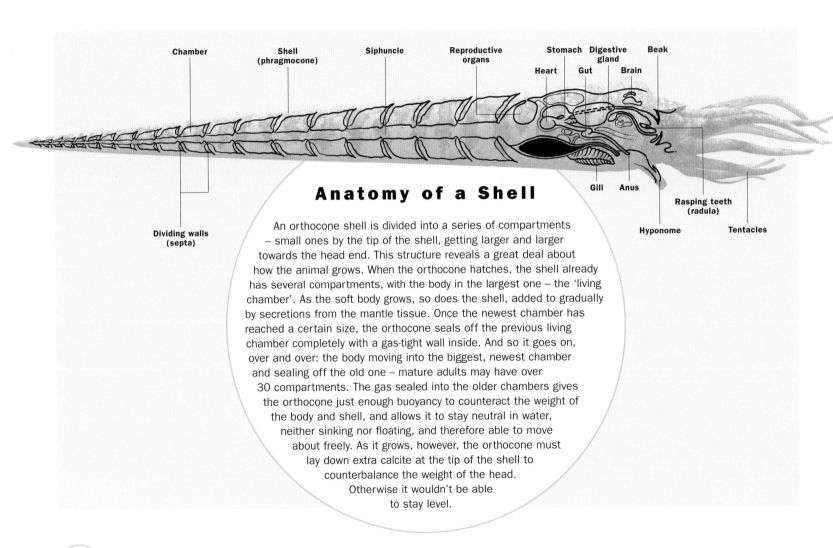

Anatomy of a Shell

An orthocone shell is divided into a series of compartments – small ones by the tip of the shell, getting larger and larger towards the head end. This structure reveals a great deal about how the animal grows. When the orthocone hatches, the shell already has several compartments, with the body in the largest one – the 'living chamber'. As the soft body grows, so does the shell, added to gradually by secretions from the mantle tissue. Once the newest chamber has reached a certain size, the orthocone seals off the previous living chamber completely with a gas-tight wall inside. And so it goes on, over and over: the body moving into the biggest, newest chamber and sealing off the old one – mature adults may have over 30 compartments. The gas sealed into the older chambers gives the orthocone just enough buoyancy to counteract the weight of the body and shell, and allows it to stay neutral in water, neither sinking nor floating, and therefore able to move about freely. As it grows, however, the orthocone must lay down extra calcite at the tip of the shell to counterbalance the weight of the head. Otherwise it wouldn't be able to stay level.

Labels: Chamber · Shell (phragmocone) · Siphuncle · Reproductive organs · Stomach · Digestive gland · Beak · Heart · Gut · Brain · Gill · Anus · Rasping teeth (radula) · Dividing walls (septa) · Hyponome · Tentacles

Blind terror

These drawbacks are no real limitation for an orthocone, because by and large their prey cannot see them coming. At this stage in prehistory, animal sight is rudimentary. Sea scorpions and trilobites have some of the most advanced vision of all, but even their eyes are restricted to seeing the difference between areas of light and dark; in the gloom of the deeper water where they hunt (around 90–180 metres/300–600 feet below the surface), they might as well be blind.

So the orthocones are successful because they exploit their main advantages – their size and their ability to sense their prey by detecting chemicals in the water. Sight is less of a factor – their pin-hole eyes are nothing like as sophisticated as they will be in later relatives such as the squid. On their tentacles are grooves (suckers haven't evolved yet) which allow them to grab their prey and then hold it firmly as they draw it into their mouth. Then it's down to the beak to finish the job: the fish may have developed armour and the sea scorpions and trilobites their tough carapaces, but the orthocone's beak is strong enough to obliterate all of them with ease.

The orthocone, then, has just what it needs to succeed as top predator. A lack of speed and poor eyesight are no handicap in a world where prey species are themselves slow and virtually blind. In the fullness of time, the picture will change considerably, as faster, more sophisticated prey emerges, pursued by faster, more sophisticated predators. Evolution is a bit like an arms race, and the Ordovician really is early days.

A torch is one useful way of discouraging an attack from an orthocone – shining it in their eyes will confuse their simple vision.

360
million years ago

The Devonian

This is the time of the very first sharks, though as yet they are not the worst things in the water – that honour belongs to dunkleosteus, a 9-metre (30-foot) long bulldozer of a fish with an armoured head and giant shearing teeth made of bone.

Age of fishes

If you wander around the aquarium section of a twenty-first-century pet shop you will see dazzling shoals of neon tetras with stripes of vivid reds and blues, and giant oscars, the size and shape of dinner plates, their dark bodies splodged with orange. Little hatchetfish, also from the Amazon, look as if they're puffing out their chests with pride, but these chests hold strong muscles for powering their fins; when attacked from below the fish fly out of the water, beating their fins a thousand times a second, faster than hummingbirds beat their wings.

The denizens of the marine section are often even flashier: gaily coloured clownfish, poster-paint orange and white, scoot in and out of the tentacles of anemones, unharmed by the stinging cells – in fact, hiding out in this poisonous forest helps protect little fishes from predators.

Other fish are venomous themselves; gaudy red and white lionfish float like galleons, confident of the protection given by their poison-tipped spines. Pufferfish, parrotfish, angels, moray eels – the variety is bewildering. There are more than 23,000 species of fish in the seas, rivers and lakes of the twenty-first century, but for all their virtues, no one would claim that fish rule the Earth. Not now anyway, but go back 360 million years and

The puffer fish, which, if attacked inflates itself with air to become a ball of spines that's very difficult to swallow, is one of the strangest-looking fish of modern times. It is nothing, however, compared to the fish of the Devonian.

The Devonian
at a glance

How bad? The fifth most dangerous sea of all time.

How long ago? 360 million years.

Where? Ohio and Montana, which at this time are sweltering on the Equator.

Shape of the continents: The world's continents are mostly concentrated into two large landmasses separated by a narrow ocean. Laurentia consists of what is now North America, western Europe and Asia, and Gondwana is made up of South America, Africa, Antarctica and Australia.

What's new? The first sharks and a frantic and marvellous explosion of other fish groups: lobe-fins, lungfishes, acanthodians and placoderms. Vertebrates are venturing on to land for the first time. The most visible change of all is on the land, which is no longer the barren, lifeless wasteland that it was in the Ordovician. The emergence of trees has produced the world's first forests, and there's a new life form in town – the insects.

THE HAZARDS

Top predator: *Dunkleosteus.*

Other predators: *Stethacanthus* ('the ironing-board shark').

Atmosphere: The good news is that the air is vastly more human-friendly: the presence of plants on land has dramatically reduced the amount of CO_2 in the air through photosynthesis and the carbon taken up by the plants to build their stems and leaves.

Day length: Although not quite as big a problem as it was in the Ordovician, jet lag would still be a problem for any humans – the Earth's spin is slowing down, but it's still much faster than in the twenty-first century, giving a day length of about 22 hours.

YOU ARE HERE

The Devonian is known as the 'Age of Fishes', because they are the dominant life form at this time.

Dunkleosteus

The terror of the Devonian seas was
Dunkleosteus a 10-metre (33 foot)
long giant from the heavily armoured
placoderm group of fish. *Dunkleosteus*
was a voracious predator whose lethal
set of slicing tooth plates would make
mince-meat of anything in its path – including
other *Dunkleosteus*!

Name: Means 'Dunkle's bones', after Dr David
Dunkle, an American palaeontologist who studied
its fossils.
Type of animal: A placoderm fish.
When was it alive? 370–360 million years ago
(Late Devonian).
Pronunciation: Dunk-lee-OWE-stee-us.
Size: 8–10 metres (25–33 feet) in length.
Diet: Fish, sharks, cephalopods and other
large animals.
Fossil finds: North America, Belgium,
Poland, Morocco.
Fact: *Dunkleosteus* didn't have
the greatest of table manners
– it would gulp down its
food and then
sometimes vomit
afterwards.

it's a different story, because now you're in the Devonian, the 'Age
of Fishes', and here the fish have more than diversity to brag about
– they are the largest predators on earth. In the Devonian the only
enemies large fish have are even larger ones.

As a scuba diver in these ancient shallow seas, you will see
significant differences between the fish you are familiar with and
those you find here. You'll meet a weird family, the placoderms, that
survived for only 50 million years; that's the equivalent of the blink of
an eye in geological time – no other fish group was around for such
a short period. You'll have the chance to swim with the sort of fish
from which all four-limbed, backboned animals, including ourselves,
are descended. And, most thrilling of all, you may come eyeball to
eyeball with a ferocious predator, easily the largest vertebrate
to evolve so far, a 9-metre (30-foot) long armour-plated
fish with jaws powerful enough to chew through metal,
and cannibalistic tendencies to boot: dunkleosteus.

Just like today, the greatest diversity of fish is found in
the warmer waters of the tropics, so you'll be heading for the
equatorial belt of the Devonian world. A single landmass, called
Laurentia, dominates the northern hemisphere. Later, forces in
the Earth's crust will break up this landmass and gradually float
the continents to where they rest today, but for now Britain and
Canada lie near the Equator. In the seas that wash these shores
there are immense coral reefs, some of them hundreds of kilometres
long, the largest structures ever built by life.

To get yourself and your equipment to the edge of this ocean,
you'll have to push your way through horsetails, club mosses and
ferns on the land. Soaring above these low-growing plants, the first
trees are outstripping the competition by growing up to 10 metres
(33 feet) tall. And there are other living things besides the plants:
spiders, mites and scorpions are proliferating, and soft-bodied
worms and centipedes have also made it ashore.

Devonian dangers

What makes this one of the most dangerous seas of all time is the giant predatory fish dunkleosteus. It doesn't have real teeth, but what it does have are just as nasty – extensions of the jaw bone that are wickedly sharp. There are two pairs of these tooth plates in the upper jaw, one pair in the lower. Cusped and serrated, during a bite they slide past each other, and this shearing action wears down the bone surfaces, keeping the cutting edges sharp. New bone is constantly being added to these weapons; in a lifetime, several centimetres of bone can be lost from self-sharpening. Powering these jaws of death are colossal muscles, giving dunkleosteus a phenomenal bite strength – its mouth is a razor-sharp vice engineered to deal with armoured prey.

Plainly, this is not the kind of place to go diving without protection. The safest way to see this animal is from within a cage. Once this is lowered into position, you enter the water and settle behind the sturdy metal bars that you hope will be dunkleosteus-proof. Try not to breathe too heavily, as bubbles from scuba tanks can frighten marine creatures away.

The view is astounding, with fragile, net-like plants floating past with the current. But look again: they're not plants, they're graptolites – giant drifting colonies of little barnacle-animals that feed on the plankton. Although human beings aren't actually descended from them, the graptolites, which became extinct about 350 million years ago, are a distant relation of the vertebrates.

A head protrudes from between some rocks: onychodus, an ambush predator that looks a bit like a moray eel. Its body stretches back 2 metres (6 feet 6 inches) into its lair. Its distensible jaws and stomach enable it to swallow prey up to half its length, so when a 1-metre (3-foot) fish swims by, quick as a flash it lunges out,

Graptolites

Small marine animals that looked a bit like modern barnacles, graptolites would join together into large colonies that would float near the sea's surface, filtering food from the ocean.

Name: Means 'written on stone', because some species look like marks made on rock.

Type of animal: A chordate, which means that they are distantly related to backboned animals such as reptiles and even mammals.

When was it alive? Between 510 and 355 million years ago (Cambrian to Devonian).

Pronunciation: Grap-toe-lite.

Size: Floating colonies could reach 1 metre (3 feet) or more in length.

Diet: Filter-feeders, eating microscopic food fragments from the water.

Fossil finds: Graptolite fossils have been found on every continent.

Fact: They may not look it, but graptolites are in fact distantly related to humans!

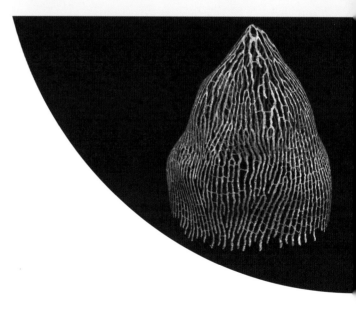

Dos and don'ts
of Devonian diving

For protection against *Dunkleosteus*, a normal shark cage
would probably not be enough. Box-shaped cages have
corners that are vulnerable to a *Dunkleosteus'* awesome bite
strength. However, there is a more dunk-proof cage design that
takes its inspiration from turtles in the southern United States.
Alligators can also bite with considerable force (equivalent to
250 kilograms per square centimetre or 1½ tonnes per square
inch), but to exert that power they need a flat object to bite down
on, otherwise their teeth slide off the target. This is why some
old turtles have grown as round as soccer balls – in the event
of an attack, the gator's teeth slide off their shells. Similarly,
if you use a spherical cage rather than a rectangular
one, *Dunkleosteus* won't be able to get any
purchase on the bars and those formidable
tooth plates will slip off the cage rather
than slicing through to the
diver inside.

As its name implies, the African lungfish is a fish with lungs that is able to live out of the water for long periods of time, so surviving droughts. Although lungfish are extremely primitive and go back some 400 million years, they were only discovered in 1836. At first European scientists refused to believe they existed, as they'd never come across a fish with lungs before.

impaling its target on whorls of dagger-like teeth. The fangs in its lower jaw are so long that they almost touch the roof of its skull. Its victim is a lobe-finned fish, a member of a major group of large Devonian-age predators. Another lobe-fin swims past your cage, giving you a good view of the two pairs of fleshy paddle-like fins beneath its body that give the group its name. It sculls along slowly, moving its fins in a motion similar to that of a four-legged land animal: each fin is composed of mobile bones and muscles to move them, and can be operated independently of the others.

The experience of seeing these lobe-finned fishes is surreal, as they're our ancestors. Just about now, on the shores of estuaries, lakes and swamps, some of these creatures are hauling out on land. All four-limbed land animals, including humans, are ultimately descended from the lobe-finned fishes. The fish sculling past could have belonged to any one of the 30 or so species that live in these waters. Only one has survived to the present day, the coelacanth, which lives in the deep waters off east and southern Africa and Indonesia.

Another group of lobe-fins reach their peak during the Devonian – the lungfish. There are many species both in salt water and in fresh water. A number of them have grinding plates in their mouths and a powerful crushing bite for cracking and breaking up hard-shelled foods, primitive clams, lamp-shells and corals. Like the coelacanth, they retain a toehold in the present day, but only half a dozen species still exist and those are all in fresh water.

The fish that will be familiar to a diver from the twenty-first century belong to another group – the ray-fins. Their fins are paper-thin with bony struts, unlike the solid bony fins of the other fish in these seas; and their long history starts here in the Devonian.

Fish out of water

At the end of the Devonian came one of the greatest break-throughs in the history of life on Earth – fish became the first backboned animals to flop on to the land. It used to be thought that they were forced into this perilous move by an arid climate desiccating their watery homes, but there's no evidence for that. In all probability it was new opportunities that lured them on to the beaches.

Oxygen is more plentiful in air than in water and there was a smorgasbord of worms, spiders and other small animals to be eaten. Escape from predators may have been another reason to get away from the water, as the seas and rivers were packed with hunters. Some of the most terrifying, up to 6 metres (20 feet) long, were a group of lobe-fins called rhizodonts, meaning 'root teeth' – their teeth extended deeply into their jaws and needed a strong base, as they were as long as the teeth of a *Tyrannosaurus rex*. Like nightmarish mudskippers, amphibious rhizodonts slithered about, stalking other fish, perhaps lurking at the top of a mud bank, using the slippery slope to slide into attack on their prey. If you could, it would make sense to watch these goings-on from the safety of dry land.

The first fishy colonists, lobe-finned fish, had developed a starter kit for survival on land while they were still swimmers. Inside their fins and body were bones, precursors of the ones in the arms, legs, shoulders and hips of

land vetebrates. These probably developed originally to improve manoeuvrability in water but helped with their first push ashore, too.

Lungs were almost in place as well. Swim bladders enable fish to regulate their vertical position in the water column, but in oxygen-deficient waters some Devonian fish used them to collect air gulped at the surface to boost their oxygen supplies, only a short evolutionary step away from a fully functioning lung.

All these features are found in *Eusthenopteron*, a fish thought to be very close to the ancestors of four-legged land animals. It could swing its forefins backwards and forwards to wiggle over the mud. Its skull is virtually identical to that of the first amphibians: *Ichthyostega* and *Acanthostega* found in Greenland, *Tulerpeton* from Russia and the

Mudskippers can spend lots of time out of the water by using their swim bladders, a trick that allowed the first fish to leave the water at the end of the Devonian.

Australian *Metaxygnathus*. These early land-lubbers made the first step on the path towards humans, albeit 360 million years ago.

Living fossils

Living fossils are plants and animals that were around in prehistoric times and survive to this day, pretty much unchanged from their ancient forms. Coelacanths and lungfish are great examples.

The coelacanth caused an earthquake in scientific circles when it was discovered in 1938. Fossils of this fish had been found, but the record ended abruptly some 70 million years ago. Then on 22 December 1938 Marjorie Courtney-Latimer, the curator of the East London Museum in South Africa, heard about an unusual fish from a haul taken near the mouth of the Chalumna River. To everyone's astonishment it turned out to be a coelacanth. It was named *Latimeria chalumnae* in honour of its discoverer and the location in which it was found.

The next coelacanth wasn't caught until 1952, in the Comoros Islands off the north-west coast of Madagascar. Since then a steady trickle of individuals has been pulled up from African waters and some have been observed undisturbed in their submarine home.

But 60 years after it was discovered, the coelacanth sprang another surprise. In 1998 a marine biologist, Mark Erdman, was on his honeymoon on the Indonesian island of Menadotua. In a bustling market he noticed a strange fish with two pairs of stumpy fins and a tail with three lobes – it couldn't have been anything but a coelacanth. The scientific world was shocked again – coelacanths had never been sighted east of Madagascar and as it turned out this was a new species that had split from the African population some 6 million years ago.

Coelacanths live on rocky reefs 150–700 metres (500–2300 feet) down but there are some spots in South Africa where they're shallow enough to dive with. They grow to almost 2 metres (6 feet 6 inches) in length and are a deep metallic blue with irregular white spots, a peculiar triple tail which generates thrust when the fishes move, and two pairs of lobed fins with which they scull through the depths. Swimming with one of these living fishes is like looking through a window into the Devonian world of 360 million years ago.

Lungfish aren't quite as famous as the coelacanth, but they're living fossils just the same. There are six species in the fresh waters of South America, Africa and Australia. All have swim bladders that act like a lung so that they can breathe air.

A coelacanth caught on camera in deep water off the Comoros Islands in the Indian Ocean. They normally shelter in caves during the day, but come out at night to feed.

The African species can survive if the pools where it lives dry up, burrowing into the mud and making itself a cocoon of mucus, which when it hardens prevents the fish from drying out. The cocoon even has a funnel to the surface of the sun-baked mud so that the lungfish can draw air into its mouth and lung.

By comparing it with fossils, scientists have established that the Australian lungfish has stayed exactly the same for at least 100 million years, making it and other lungfish some of the most durable vertebrates known on Earth.

Cheirolepis is a typical predator of this group; the bones in its skull are loosely attached, just like a snake's, so they can move freely in relation to each other. The skull can virtually come apart when the jaws open, so cheirolepis can gulp down large prey, up to two-thirds its own length. For the moment ray-fins seem insignificant compared to the other flamboyant fish groups around, but their time will come.

The first fish to evolve – about 450 million years ago, though some controversial bone-like fragments found in Cambrian rocks may push this date back another 100 million years or so – were all jawless. It took about 100 million years for the explosion of fishes you see in the Devonian to happen, and for most of that time fish survived perfectly well without jaws, hoovering up food trapped in sediments or using their sucker mouths to rasp away flesh from the dead or dying. Most jawless fish will be extinct by the end of the Devonian, probably outcompeted by fish with jaws.

There are many small predators in these oceans, but you are really here to see a dunkleosteus. Using another fish as bait could draw one in. Stirring up the seabed, you discover a fish as curious as anything you have seen so far – a bothriolepis. Its head is broad and flat with a few tough plates like shields, and to complete this armour there are smaller plates between the larger ones. The back half is flexible, covered in a mesh of small scales, and the fish

Bothriolepis

A small species of placoderm and thus distantly related to *Dunkleosteus*. Much of *Bothriolepis'* time would have been spent on the seabed where it ate small crustaceans and other invertebrates.

Name: Means 'pitted scale'.
Type of animal: A placoderm fish.
When was it alive? 380–355 million years ago (Mid to Late Devonian).
Pronunciation: BOTH-ree-oh-lep-is.
Size: 30 centimetres–1.5 metres (1–5 feet) in length.
Diet: Worms and other small seabed animals.
Fossil finds: Europe, East Asia, Australia, Africa, North America and Antarctica.
Fact: *Bothriolepis* was probably on the menu of every large predator during the Late Devonian.

A bothriolepis doing what it does best – moving slowly along the seabed, sifting through the sediment for food.

Stethacanthus

Sometimes also called 'the ironing-board shark' because of its strange-shaped dorsal fin, *Stethacanthus* looked and behaved much like many modern reef sharks and would have hunted fish and other swimming animals.

Name: Means 'chest spine'.
Type of animal: A primitive member of the shark family.
When was it alive? 370–345 million years ago (Late Devonian to Late Carboniferous).
Pronunciation: STETH-ac-anth-us.

Size: 70 centimetres–2 metres (2 feet 3 inches–6 feet 6 inches) in length.
Diet: Small fish and cephalopods.
Fossil finds: North America, Scotland, France, Russia and Poland.
Fact: The strange ironing-board-shaped dorsal fin may have been used to attract females or to frighten potential predators – viewed from the front it might have made the shark look as if it had a gigantic mouth.

moves forward by thrashing its tail from side to side. Fortunately, it is not fast-moving and from the side of the cage a spear-gun aimed at the soft part of its body is enough to catch the bait you need. When you flip the bothriolepis over, you find only a simple slit for a mouth, which it uses to grub along the seabed.

The bothriolepis seeps blood into the water and it's that blood trail that will attract dunkleosteus. But fish blood in tropical seas entices other hunters too, creatures that can detect one molecule of blood in a million of water – sharks.

First sharks

Cladoselache, the earliest known form of shark, has just appeared in the Late Devonian. About 2 metres (6 feet 6 inches) long and at first glance not so very different from the sharks of today, it has wide pectoral fins that flare out from the front of its body, helping it manoeuvre with pinpoint accuracy. In the final lunge for prey, mainly small fish, it is powered by a deep tail sweeping from side to side. Its body is topped by two dorsal fins, the front one preceded by a stout spine, a feature not seen in contemporary sharks. There are other more subtle differences too.

Modern sharks have a tooth factory in their mouths: a system like a conveyor belt in the gums keeps bringing new sharp teeth to replace blunt or broken ones. A small lemon shark can go through 10,000 teeth in its ten-year lifespan. Cladoselache doesn't have such a sophisticated system and its teeth can sometimes be worn down to stubs. Also, its jaws are weak and poorly developed compared to those of modern sharks. The basic shark design was pretty good right from the start, but over 400 million years tiny improvements

Stethacanthus, or 'the ironing-board shark', is one of the earliest species of shark. Only the males have the characteristic anvil-like fin on their back, the top of which is covered in tooth-shaped scales. The function of its fin remains a bit of a mystery. Was it to attract females or did it intimidate rivals by looking like a giant mouth from the front?

such as more resilient teeth and more effective streamlining have enhanced their ability to hunt and feed.

In the Devonian seas, however, there are 'off the wall' sharks, unlike any others coming before or after them. Palaeontologists call one of the strangest stethacanthus, but its colloquial name is 'the ironing-board shark'. The males of this extraordinary species have a dorsal fin in the shape of an ironing-board adorned with a brush of teeth along the flattened top. This tooth-covered pedestal is probably used to impress females during courtship.

Sharks are always mesmerizing. As you can't take your eyes off them, you will soon notice that they've suddenly skedaddled. Why? Because of a giant that with one snap could slice a shark in two. Dunkleosteus has arrived at last.

The original 'Jaws'

Dunkleosteus is the ultimate placoderm. The name placoderm derives from the Greek for 'plated skin' and members of the group all have armour plating – 5 centimetres (2 inches) thick in case of dunkleosteus, although it is armoured only on the front part of its body. It is certainly in need of a protective covering; many individuals have scars on their bodies. So these monsters either have serious skirmishes when feeding or, as happens in some species of fish, larger ones cannibalize smaller ones.

The smell of the bait fish soon proves irresistible and the dunkleosteus, all 9 metres (30 feet) of it, surges forwards. As it accelerates towards the cage, a shoal of smaller fish silvered in the sunlight scatters ahead of it. Their most striking features are bodies that bristle with bony spines. These jawed fish, belonging to a group called acanthodians, are abundant in the fossil record.

Placoderms

A beautifully preserved *Dunkleosteus* fossil from the Cleveland Museum of Natural History. The hard plates in its head survive fossilization, but the rest of the body doesn't.

The evolutionary success story of the Devonian period was arguably the placoderm group of fish. They first evolved at the very end of the Silurian period, about 410 million years ago, but within a few million years they had taken over from the jawless fish to become the most dominant and widespread fish on Earth.

The placoderms' success came about for a number of reasons. First, they evolved a layer of armour plating that covered their head and shoulders, providing protection against predators such as the sea scorpions. Also of great importance were their jaws, which enabled them to handle different types of food and actively to hunt large prey. There is also strong evidence that they were the first backboned animals to indulge in sexual intercourse, which is known to be an efficient reproductive strategy. These, and many other minor factors, gave the placoderms the edge over the jawless fish whose numbers declined dramatically during the Devonian.

There were many different types of placoderm fish, and *Dunkleosteus* was one of the strangest and deadliest of them all. Looking like a cross between a giant eel and an armour-plated tank, *Dunkleosteus* was a living nightmare, capable of attacking anything in its path. Most placoderms were only 1 metre (3 feet) or so in length, but *Dunkleosteus* could grow to 10 metres (33 feet), making it the largest predator in the Devonian seas. As if this wasn't bad enough, *Dunkleosteus* had another feature that made it deadlier yet. Instead of having teeth, like sharks and other fish, on each jaw, it had two razor-sharp plates that would clamp down on any prey, slicing them cleanly in two (a bit like a guillotine). Once caught in these

jaws, few animals would have been able to struggle free again. Because it didn't have proper teeth, it probably ate by swallowing its prey in huge chunks. Sometimes this was too much for its stomach and it would vomit back its dinner on to the seabed. Fossils of *Dunkleosteus* vomit (scientists call them palaeolags) are a common find and by looking at them we can see that this predator was not fussy about its food. Anything that swam in the sea or crawled on the seabed would have been on the menu – fish, sharks, sea scorpions, cephalopods, you name it. There is even evidence that *Dunkleosteus* was a cannibal and that individuals regularly attacked each other, leaving deep scars on their armour-plating.

Not that *Dunkleosteus* had it all its own way. One fossil shows one that tried to swallow another large fish whole, tail first. A spine on the back of this fish got stuck in the roof of the *Dunkleosteus'* mouth, puncturing a hole through to its brain and killing it.

Although it had size and power on its side, *Dunkleosteus* was not the most successful of all the placoderms, due to its weighty, inflexible and unsophisticated design. This honour probably went to the

small and rather inoffensive *Bothriolepis*, which lived by sifting mud for worms and other invertebrates. The key to *Bothriolepis'* success was its adaptability. Its fossils have been found on every continent, including Antarctica, over a 30-million-year time range, and in almost every environment: the sea, lakes, estuaries and rivers. There is even evidence that some species had primitive lungs, allowing them to breathe air for short periods of time. This ability to find and exploit new environments kept *Bothriolepis* ahead of its rivals, including *Dunkleosteus*, and ensured that it was a familiar part of the Devonian landscape.

The end of the Devonian saw many new types of fish evolve and diversify. The sharks, ray-fins (ancestors to most modern fish) and lobe-finned fish (such as the coelacanths) were all fast-moving and adaptable. Soon they were outcompeting the placoderms, leading to their slow decline. Even *Bothriolepis* could not withstand the pace of change and, like all other placoderms, vanished from the fossil record around 355 million years ago. After a reign of over 60 million years the plate-skinned fish had been assigned to the pages of geological history.

You should be able to get a good view of a dunkleosteus from inside your diving cage. If one tries to bite through the bars, its jaws should slip off the spherical sides.

Quite modern-looking, they reach a peak of diversity in the Devonian period, dying out at the close of the Permian, some 250 million years ago. Dunkleosteus ignores these little fish – it has its eye on more substantial prey. To maximize its gape it lifts its head, simultaneously dropping its lower jaw, slamming against the cage and swallowing the 1-metre (3-foot) long bothriolepis in one go. Jaws first arose in fish through the modification of the slender bones in the throat region that supported the gill arches. In dunkleosteus they are considerably more advanced and give a striking illustration of how possessing jaws brings huge advantages, opening up a whole new menu of possible prey. Larger animals can be seized and manipulated, even disabled by a lightning-fast strike. Once caught, the victim can be cut or crushed with precision.

Sound travels farther and faster in water than in air, so from your diving cage you can clearly hear dunkleosteus chomping its meal. Most of its food is armour-plated, hence the bony shears in its mouth. Imagine the sound of the bothriolepis being cracked open. Fingernails scraping down a blackboard are nothing compared to that; it would be a thousand times more effective at putting your teeth on edge.

There's still a stomach-churning sight to come. The great body of the dunkleosteus shudders and shakes. Suddenly the indigestible parts of its meal are regurgitated in a cloud. Its formidable teeth may be able to crush through the armour of bothriolepis, but its stomach can only process the softer parts – once it has digested what it can, the rest is rejected. The acanthodian shoal darts through this spew of shards of fish armour, on the look-out for fleshy morsels amongst the hard bits. The giant from whose table they're seeking scraps turns and, with one great sweep of its tail, disappears out of sight.

Fragments of dunkleosteus vomit have been found in fossil records. It appears that they regurgitated indigestible bits of their meals, just like owls and falcons do today, but in dunkleosteus' case they'd spew out armour plate and bones from their fish prey.

What you see on one dive like this just scratches the surface of the diversity of Devonian fish, but that variety won't last long. In 5 million years there will be a major extinction in the oceans and 35 out of the 46 families of fishes alive will become extinct, including the jawless fish, the majority of the placoderms (though a few will hang on for another 5 million years), the acanthodians and most of the lobe-fins – all will be gone.

The waters will be dominated by the sharks and a group that seems insignificant here in the Devonian – the ray-fins, who will survive to become the most abundant living fishes. Those tetras, oscars, hatchetfish, clownfish and scorpionfish in the pet shop are all ray-fins. How different it would be wandering around the aquarium section if there were still placoderms and acanthodians, although it would be a brave aquarist who took on a dunkleosteus, even a baby one. Not that many scuba divers would be thinking about the demise of the acanthodians with a dunkleosteus waiting in the gloom.

230
million years ago

The Triassic

Before the Triassic, fish had dominated the oceans. But then the reptiles moved from land into the water and a whole gamut of previously unknown marine predators started to terrorize sea life, including tanystropheus (pictured) and the 10-metre (33-foot) long cymbospondylus.

Out of the blue

With a thunderous crash a wave rolls on to an ancient beach. Exploiting its impetus, monsters materialize from the ocean. As the water recedes in a gurgling mass of foam and sand, three are left behind. Their damp, scaly bodies glisten in the moonlight as they begin a laborious crawl up the beach. These are nothosaurs, a group of reptiles that will flourish and diversify throughout the Triassic, but will then die out.

The reptiles can move only slowly, using large front flippers to push and pull themselves forward. Above the strandline, the sloping beach isn't smooth any more. Instead, it's pock-marked with newly dug craters and depressions – sea-monster nests.

The trio of slowly advancing nothosaurs are all females and they have come here to lay their eggs. As the first one crosses the strand line, her long tail makes a swathe through the washed-up debris – cast skins of horseshoe crabs, dried-up jellyfish, algae bleached by the sun and fragments of sea-urchin shells.

The females must get above the reach of the highest tides before laying, otherwise their eggs could be inundated by salt water and then the precious embryos inside would perish.

Nothosaur

As amphibious reptiles, nothosaurs were perfectly at home in the sea but could come out on to land from time to time. They probably hunted much like modern seals, hunting for fish and other animals in shallow coastal waters.

Name: Means 'false lizard'.
Type of animal: A member of the nothosauria group of marine reptiles.
When was it alive? 240–210 million years ago (Triassic).
Pronunciation: NOTH-oh-sawr.
Size: Up to 4 metres (13 feet) in length.
Diet: An ambush predator, feeding on fish, cephalopods and small reptiles.

Fossil finds: Asia, Europe and North Africa.
Fact: Nothosaurs may have been keen sunbathers, hauling themselves on to the land so that they could bask in the sun's rays.

YOU ARE HERE

From mountain range to coastline – the Swiss Alps as they appear in the Triassic. Scientists will study marine fossils from here in 230 million years.

dry climate has heavily influenced the plant life, allowing hardy conifers, cycads, ginkgos and ferns to dominate the land.

The Triassic at a glance

How bad? The sixth most dangerous sea of all time.

How long ago? 230 million years.

Where? The Swiss Alps, which at this time are a shallow tropical sea near the ancient European coastline.

Shape of the continents: The world is dominated by the giant supercontinent Pangea (meaning 'all the land'), which is made of all the other world's continents squashed together. Pangea lies in the centre of the globe, stretching in a line from the Arctic to the Antarctic and is surrounded by the vast Panthalassa Ocean (meaning 'all the seas'). The bunching of the continents creates a phenomenon whereby one hemisphere of the globe consists solely of ocean, the other only of land.

What's new? The global climate is warm and dry, causing huge sandy deserts in the centre of Pangea and confining much of life to the edge of the continent, where the sea breezes provide much-needed moisture. Life on Earth is just beginning to recover from a gigantic extinction event that occurred only 20 million years ago. The reptiles are in control of the land and the earliest types of dinosaur, crocodile and pterosaur are just evolving, as are the cynodonts. The reptiles have also entered the sea and have overtaken the sharks and other fish to become the top predators there. The

THE HAZARDS

Top predator: *Cymbospondylus*

Other predators: Nothosaurs, *Tanystropheus*.

On shore: This is of course the time of the very first dinosaurs, but the good news is that they haven't yet got to the staggering sizes for which they will become so famous. A typical dinosaur species around here is the *Coelurosaur*, which is no more than 2– 3 metres (6–10 feet)in length. The real concern on land is the vicious *Prestosuchus* – a 5-metre (16-foot) long reptile and the largest carnivore on land at this time.

Nothosaurs have to come ashore to lay eggs, just like modern-day sea turtles. It's likely the males gathered in the shallows just off the breeding beaches to mate with the females.

Clouds of sand explode upwards; other nothosaurs are already digging – there are at least a dozen on a stretch of beach only 100 metres (300 feet) long. The first of the three females picks her spot; the other two choose theirs to her left. There's no co-operation here – it's each female for herself. Sometimes they even accidentally uncover a clutch of previously buried eggs, which will then spoil or be eaten by predators. The first female begins flailing her flippers to evacuate a chamber in the sand. At sea she uses them as rudders, but now they do just fine as spades, although the work is laborious as loose sand keeps sliding down the sides of her pit.

Taking a break between spates of digging, she rests her dragon-like head on the sand, blowing a thin shower of water droplets from her nostrils. These sneezes aren't caused by a head cold. Out at sea nothosaurs can't avoid taking in excess salt with their food and even though reptiles can tolerate quite large fluctuations in the composition of their body fluids, there's a limit. The nothosaur eliminates salt by means of a gland which absorbs the excess from her blood; she can then snort it out in a salty spray.

She digs and rests, digs and rests. Just before she has completed her task, a shape shuffles across the sand towards her. She opens her mouth full of interlocking teeth, to hiss a warning, but it's only another nothosaur, heading back down the beach to the sea after laying her eggs. The female's own sandpit is now deep enough, some 60 centimetres (2 feet) deep, and she slides forward, kinking the back of her body down into the hole. Leathery-shelled eggs the size of ping-pong balls begin to plop into the nest from her cloaca, her joint opening for excretory and reproductive organs. She lays a clutch of eggs and then uses her back legs to fill in the hole and cover them. That is the extent of her maternal duties – the eggs are on their own now and with luck, incubated by the warmth of the sun, her babies will hatch out in a couple of months' time.

The shells of reptile eggs are much more leathery and pliable than the hard chalky shells of birds' eggs.

Dragons at sea

Her exertion over, the nothosaur turns and heads towards the breaking surf. The sky glows orange, and by the time the first wave breaks over her back she looks even more dragon-like, her scales fiery with the light from the risen sun.

Plunging beneath the surface, we're about to join her on a prehistoric voyage. We're about 230 million years before the twenty-first century. In Triassic times there is one great southern continent (which will become known as Gondwana when it breaks away at the start of the Jurassic) jostling together with the northern one (Laurasia), forming the supercontinent Pangea. Most of the world's landmass lies in the equatorial belt, so climates follow a similar pattern in much of what will become North America, Europe, Africa, India and Australia: hot and dry most of the time, with an annual wet season to resuscitate the land. Although there are no big dinosaurs yet, reptiles reign supreme. On the land there are large and small ones, plant-eaters that are prey for meat-eaters. Some live on high ground, some along watercourses, others in trees. But perhaps because there was so much competition for food and territory, many reptiles have moved out to sea.

The female nothosaur is much more graceful in water than she was on the land. On the beach her body had the appearance of being concertinaed together, but now, supported in water and fully unfurled, its design can be appreciated. The toothy head is small compared to the elongated neck and body. Streaming behind, the tail makes up half the total length of 4 metres (13 feet 6 inches); undulating the tail propels the nothosaur through the water, while steering is achieved with her paddle-like forelimbs and back legs.

She's hungry, and after taking a breath of air at the surface she

The toothy array in a nothosaur's mouth is ideal for gaffing fish and squid, the mainstay of their diet.

The genesis
of the dinosaurs

The beginning of the Mesozoic era is marked by a great extinction event that killed off 95 per cent of all animal life on Earth. Only a handful of reptile species survived, including a group called the archosauriformes. Before the extinction the archosauriformes had been an insignificant part of life. Afterwards they were to give rise to some of the most terrifying creatures ever to walk the Earth.

Some 250 million years ago the largest archosauriforme was only 1 metre (3 feet) or so in length, but they evolved fast and within a few million years had split into three of the most important reptile groups of all time: the crocodiles, the pterosaurs and the dinosaurs. These would grow rapidly in number and size and would dominate the world for the rest of the Mesozoic era.

The oldest dinosaur fossils are around 230–225 million years old, dating from the late Triassic. Even at this early stage the dinosaurs were to be found on all the continents except Antarctica, which means that they probably evolved earlier, perhaps around 235–240 million years ago.

The record for the world's oldest dinosaur fossil used go to *Herrerasaurus*, a 227-million-year-old dinosaur from Argentina, but more recent finds in Brazil and Madagascar seem to be older, though need to be verified. It would appear that the most primitive dinosaurs belonged to one of two subgroups: the theropods (two-legged meat-eaters such as *Tyrannosaurus rex*) and the prosauropods (large herbivores that would eventually give rise to the giant sauropods such as *Diplodocus*).

The dinosaurs wasted no time in their quest for global domination. For the remainder of the Triassic era the dinosaurs increased in number and size, evolving new species and spreading themselves across the globe. Their big break came at the end of the Triassic when, after a minor extinction event, the number of dinosaurs started to increase rapidly until, by the early Jurassic, they were the largest and most dominant reptile on Earth. They remained in charge until their famed and sudden extinction 65 million years ago. The birds, who are the dinosaurs' direct descendents, are all that remains of these mighty beasts.

Early dinosaurs were not nearly as big as their successors; some later species reached 40 metres (130 feet) in length.

Like all marine reptiles, nothosaurs have to come to the surface to breathe. Their nostrils are located on the top of their snouts to make taking a breath easier.

speeds towards a shoal of silvery fish. The dense bones of her skeleton act as ballast to keep her below the surface. Taking evasive action, the shoal explodes every which way, but with her elongated, supple body and jaws lined with needle-like teeth, just perfect for gaffing fish, the nothosaur impales two or three and swallows them. One fish just gets away after being strafed by her teeth – badly injured, it spirals down towards a bed of weeds.

There's another nothosaur concealed in the weeds. It grabs this manna from heaven, but even though the fish is injured, it's still a struggle for the reptile, because this is a tiny species of nothosaur; an adult neuticosaurus is only 18 centimetres (8 inches) long, but the fish into which it's embedded its teeth is 15 centimetres (6 inches) long – only a little bit shorter. Fish and reptile tussle like horse and cowboy in a bucking-bronco competition, but eventually the prey is subdued and dragged back into the weeds, where the miniature sea monster dismembers it into bite-sized chunks.

Unmoved by the disturbance caused by her leftovers, the larger nothosaur swims languidly in the sun-warmed surface waters; she's a reptile and needs this warmth to help digest her meal.

Below her, attached to the rocks, is a vast bed of shellfish. Using strong talons to anchor themselves in the surge, half a dozen fat, lizard-like reptiles gorge on the molluscs. These are placodonts, another group of Triassic marine reptiles that left no descendants.

Placodonts specialize in shellfish. One is feeding right below the nothosaur, its short, broad head buried in the bed of shellfish, detaching a mollusc with a jiggle and a jerk. It winkles its food from the rocks with long teeth at the front of its mouth, but it still has to break the shell to reach the soft-bodied animal inside. The rear teeth – flat, broad and covered with heavy enamel – act as millstones; with these the placodont crushes the hard, heavy shell. After spitting out the splinters which stream away in the current it swallows the fleshy parts that remain.

Sticking its neck out

The nothosaur's scaly eyes are shut. She's snoozing, but not for long; she's about to be woken by the most preposterous marine reptile that's ever lived – tanystropheus. Instinctively she dives, but as it's a tanystropheus, not a predator, she's unconcerned and with a flick of her tail she's back at the surface. The reptile that disturbed her is nearly 6 metres (20 feet) long, a clumsy swimmer with sprawling legs and clawed feet. Its stupendously long neck, comprising more than half the creature's length is what makes it bizarre. Like a giraffe, this boom-like neck doesn't have large numbers of vertebrae to support it (giraffes, like humans, have seven neck vertebrae). Tanystropheus has just a dozen, but they're huge, each up to 30 centimetres (12 inches) long. This fact, combined with comparatively weak musculature, means the neck is stiff and inflexible. So what is a neck like that for?

The tanystropheus plants its feet firmly on some rocks in the shallows, its neck held out straight like a rod, its body disguised among the silt and stone. Before long shoals of fish swim around the rocks and over the sand, oblivious to any danger. Suddenly the reptile swoops its neck down and to the side, scattering the shoal which regroups a safe distance away – one fish down.

Tanystropheus

This reptile's most distinctive feature was its phenomenally long neck which presented it with all types of problems when swimming and walking. However, it probably came in handy when stalking shoals of fish.

Name: Means 'long vertebra'.
Type of animal: An extinct type of prolacertiform reptile.
When was it alive? 235–210 million years ago (Late Triassic).
Pronunciation: TAN-ee-STRO-fee-us.
Size: 6 metres (20 feet) in length.
Diet: Small fish and cephalopods.

Fossil finds: Asia and Europe.
Fact: Engineers have calculated that *Tanystropheus* has the longest neck length permissible under the laws of physics!

Cymbospondylus

The marine reptile *Cymbospondylus* was a gigantic type of ichthyosaur that used its powerful streamlined body to hunt down prey in shallow water.

Name: Means 'boat vertebrae'.

Type of animal: An early member of the extinct ichthyosaur group of marine reptiles.

When was it alive? 240–210 million years ago (Late Triassic).

Pronunciation: Sim-bow-SPOND-ee-lus.

Size: 10 metres (33 feet) in length.

Diet: Fish, cephalopods and possibly other marine reptiles.

Fossil finds: North America and Europe.

Fact: One of the largest ichthyosaurs ever to have evolved, it ruled the Triassic seas.

The tanystropheus moves slowly off into deeper water to continue its hunting. Swimming gently, it approaches a shoal. It can make a close approach with its relatively small head because, as it is extended so far away from the body, the fish don't associate it with the bulky body and aren't spooked. Once it feels it is close enough, the predator swings its head sideways, ending up with a fish wiggling in its jaws. Two possible uses for the long neck there – sneaking up on prey, and then less drag when you swing your head through the water for a catch. In the twenty-first century, gharials – fish-eating crocodiles found in India – have a long and tapered snout for this reason: there's much less drag when they swing it through a shoal of fast-moving fish than if they had a short, broad snout like an alligator.

The fish shoal that attracted tanystropheus lures the nothosaur, too, and she's joined by others of her kind. It's late afternoon now and females that haven't yet laid their eggs are gathering close to the beach, ready to make their nocturnal crawl above the strandline. Fish are snaffled up everywhere, as the predators feast on their prey.

Fish scales reign down to the seafloor, shimmering like giant silver raindrops in the slanting rays of the afternoon sun. Suddenly a fast-moving shape 6 metres (20 feet) long – half as large again as the nothosaurs – races out from behind a coral head. It's a cymbospondylus, one of the earliest ichthyosaurs or 'fish lizards'. Of all of the marine reptiles, ichthyosaurs are the most striking example of adaptation to a completely aquatic way of life. There are no reptiles in the Triassic or at any time in the future that can live permanently beneath the waves – all reptiles must come to the surface to breathe and even fish extract oxygen directly from the water. As the nothosaurs scatter in front of the cymbospondylus, it shows all the classic ichthyosaur features. Its body is sleek and

Giant ichthyosaurs

At 10 metres (33 feet) in length, the Triassic ichthyosaur *Cymbospondylus* was truly gigantic in comparison to modern marine life. It was, however, a mere minnow when compared to other Triassic ichthyosaurs.

The largest formally identified ichthyosaur is *Shonisaurus*, whose remains were first found near the Nevada town of Berlin in 1928. This monster grew to over 15 metres (50 feet) in length and could weigh 40 tonnes – that's about the same size as an adult sperm whale. In fact, *Shonisaurus* was so large that local miners allegedly used its individual bones as dinner plates.

Shonisaurus had a classical Triassic ichthyosaur shape – a sleek aquiline body, powerful tail and long, thin snout full of sharp, pointed teeth. It was most likely a fish-eater, pursuing its prey at speed through the shallow waters that covered ancient Nevada. The quarry in which *Shonisaurus* was originally found has also produced over 30 other giant ichthyosaur skeletons. This has

led to the idea that they may have become stranded on an ancient beach. Another theory is that they simply died of natural causes and that over time their skeletons sank to the seabed.

For years *Shonisaurus* was believed to be the largest ichthyosaur. Then, in 1991, a Canadian archaeologist looking for historical artefacts stumbled across a gigantic set of bones in a remote riverbed in a British Columbian forest. The skeleton belonged to an ichthyosaur that was a staggering 23 metres (75 feet) long. Its head alone was 6 metres (20 feet) in length, which is longer than a killer whale.

The remoteness of the fossil has meant that it has taken several years to remove it from the rock

A giant ichthyosaur is exhumed, high up a mountain in the Nevada desert in America in 1953. Leading the excavation is Dr Charles Camp (centre).

and it has yet to receive a formal name. This unnamed sea monster lived around 210 million years ago, slightly more recently than *Shonisaurus*. This means that the two could never have met, but that is perhaps just as well.

Cymbospondylus don't normally take large prey, preferring mainly fish and squid, but Nigel isn't taking any chances, using an electric prod to keep the ichthyosaur at bay.

streamlined, its tail – the propulsive force behind its surging movements – sweeping from side to side. It is bent slightly downwards at the back with a fin along the lower half (later ichthyosaurs will have a heterocercal tail just like a fish's). At the front the neck is so short it can barely be seen. Clearing the water, with just a few bubbles spinning away to show the speed, is a long head with a sharp snout with a hundred sharp teeth on each side of the jaw.

The tanystropheus doesn't react quickly enough and the cymbospondylus points its body like a missile at its prey. It makes contact halfway along the tail and there's a puff of blood. The ichthyosaur's teeth rip through its prey's flesh. You would have thought that this must be the end, but then out of the red cloud the tanystropheus swims to safety. It has shed its tail to escape, a trick that's used by many modern-day lizards too. The escape mechanism relies on many of the tail vertebrae having fracture lines, so that they break apart if their owner is attacked and the tail is sacrificed to distract the predator. A replacement

Autotomy is the technical term for tail shedding, a diversionary tactic used by many lizards and some salamanders when they're attacked from behind, giving them time to escape. The tails regrow, as you can see with this lizard, but they're never as prefect as the original.

From the side you can see the amazing shape of the tanystropheus' body. They often hide in the coral with just their slender necks sticking out, ready to ambush passing fish.

tail usually grows with time. The muscles in the tail still work after it's been dropped and now the one that used to belong to the tanystropheus thrashes violently in the jaws of the cymbospondylus.

The attack isn't a complete waste of effort for the ichthyosaur, however – in fact this is quite a substantial meal, for this is a pregnant female and her usual diet is small fish and squid. Unlike nothosaurs, ichthyosaurs don't go ashore to nest. Instead they give birth to live young at sea and this one has foetuses growing inside her.

The female nothosaur who laid her eggs on the beach last night cruised away to safety during the attack on the tanystropheus. She's swimming down after more victims in a small school of fish. Tomorrow she'll drift away from the area of the nesting beach – she's laid all her eggs for this season and until the next one there are richer feeding grounds than this.

Running the gauntlet

Some two months later there are stirrings beneath the sand in the nothosaur's nest. More than 50 miniature sea monsters have hatched and moving together they force their way upwards, erupting out at the surface. Over the next 15 minutes the young nothosaurs face a time of great peril, probably more than at any other time in their life. As they head for the lighter horizon over the sea, their trip over the sand to the surf must be both fast and direct.

One hunter attracted by the movements in the sand looms over the nest as the hatchlings break out. It's waddled out from swampy ground behind the beach. Mastodonsaurus is one of the largest amphibians ever to have lived, 4 metres (13 feet) long from its snout to the tip of its tail. (The largest amphibian alive today is the Asian giant salamander, a mere 1.7 metres/5 feet 6 inches long.) You'd

Marine reptiles today

Marine reptiles had their zenith in the Mesozoic era. For over 165 million years the oceans were jam-packed with a constantly changing cast of nothosaurs, placodonts, ichthyosaurs, plesiosaurs, sea-going crocodiles and turtles. Today our marine reptile fauna has much less variety. Even so, there are species just as fascinating as those from prehistoric seas. And I (Nigel Marven) have been lucky enough to encounter one or two of them.

Nowadays only a few species of crocodiles venture out to sea: in the Americas the rare American, Cuban and Morelet's crocodiles often live in coastal habitats and may even island-hop. The saltwater crocodile of Australasia, which can grow to 7 metres (23 feet) long, lives up to its name – sort of! It's commonly encountered in marine habitats and can survive well in the open ocean, colonizing small islands such as the Cocos Islands nearly 1000 kilometres (625 miles) from the mainland, although just as often it's found in freshwater habitats, large rivers and lakes.

The only sea-loving lizard today is the remarkable marine iguana from the Galapagos. One of my sweetest moments was diving down with mask and snorkel just 1 metre (3 feet) or so below the surface, in the surging water just off the boulder-strewn coast of the island of Fernandina. The rip was so strong that it was all I could do to hold on to a sharp volcanic rock, but hold on I did, because only the width of my dive mask away a marine iguana was grazing on algae. Surely the inspiration for the movie monster Godzilla, it boasted jet-black scales and a comb of spines just behind its head. I could hear the sound of its three-cusped razor-sharp teeth scraping seaweed from the rocks.

The saltwater crocodiles of Australasia can tackle prey as large as water buffalo. Their peg-like teeth are for grasping, not cutting, which is why crocodiles spin and roll in the water to dismember their prey.

The marine iguana is the only species of lizard that lives in and next to the ocean. It even relies on the sea for its food – algae.

The reptile kept position in the powerful currents, using its long, sharp claws like grappling irons. It was an unforgettable sight. I came up for air and dived down to watch the iguana again and again – it didn't take a breath for the whole of the time it was feeding, eight minutes or so. Then both of us swam back to shore to warm up in the sun.

These lizards live in colonies and as I sunbathed I was surrounded by piles of iguanas doing the same. They ingest large amounts of salt when feeding and get rid of the excess using a gland between their eyes and nose which opens out into their nostrils. Every so often the lizards snorted

explosively, shooting a salty spray into the air. They also sneeze like this to warn intruders off and I was sprayed whenever I got too close.

There's another extraordinary sea-going reptile that I haven't had the pleasure of meeting, although it's high on my wish list. It's huge, averaging 1.5 metres (5 feet) long and weighing in between 200 and 700 kilograms (440 and 1550 pounds). The largest ever recorded was 2.6 metres (8 feet 6 inches) long and weighed 914 kilograms (2015 pounds); it was found stranded off the west coast of Wales in 1988. This creature can stay underwater for two hours and can dive down to 1200 metres (4000 feet). Surprisingly it sustains its great bulk on foods that are 99 per cent water – jellyfish, comb jellies and tonicates – probably getting enough of these to eat by diving in deep waters and zeroing in on the bio-luminescent glow of jellyfish in the darkness. I'm talking about the leatherback turtle, the largest of the eight species of turtle in our oceans today.

All these modern marine reptiles must come ashore to lay their eggs. The venomous sea snakes, however, are so perfectly adapted to life in the oceans that they almost never touch land. Of the 50 or so species, only the four sea kraits, which live in the waters of South-East Asia and the south-western Pacific Islands, come ashore to lay eggs; the rest are live-bearers, giving birth in the open ocean. Depending on the species, six to 20 young are born underwater, and are independent from the start – the babies surface for their first breath and must begin to catch fish instinctively within a week or so.

I've encountered only one species of sea snake – *Pelamis*, in the warm waters of Oman. Floating at the surface was an adult some 60 centimetres (2 feet) long, a gaudy reptilian ribbon, vivid yellow below, jet black above, with a river of yellow meandering along the paddle-shaped tail. The snake took a breath and dived effortlessly. It was only a tantalizing glimpse, but even though I was wearing scuba gear, I wouldn't have kept up for long if I'd tried to follow this beauty. These

The banded sea krait is still tied to the land. It must come ashore to lay its eggs – there are up to a dozen in each clutch.

reptiles swim vertically downwards at a rate of 1 metre (3 feet) every three seconds and they can dive 200 metres (650 feet) down. The only chance for a close-up underwater view is if they come to investigate you. Although their venom is highly toxic, they're docile and phlegmatic, rarely biting people unless they're grabbed or hurt. Some sea snakes have venom as toxic as all but the most venomous and dangerous of land snakes and can deliver enough in a single bite to kill thousands of mice. They need such powerful venom to immobilize their prey quickly, reducing the risk of injury to the snake and the chance of the fish swimming away.

Pelamis has a phenomenal range – its territory extends from the waters off eastern Africa, along the coast of southern Asia, through the Australian archipelago, northward to Japan, south along the eastern coast of Australia and eastward across the Pacific as far as the western coast of the Americas. If the sea is unusually calm, *Pelamis* sometimes gather together in a mass that can span tens of metres of the sea's surface. But that's nothing compared to an aggregation of the sea snake *Astrotia*, recorded in the Malacca Strait in 1932. A nearly solid mass of a million snakes, many of them intertwined, formed a line 3 metres (10 feet) wide and 100 kilometres (62 miles) long. What a phenomenal sighting that would be – as terrific a spectacle as many of the sea monsters of the past could have provided.

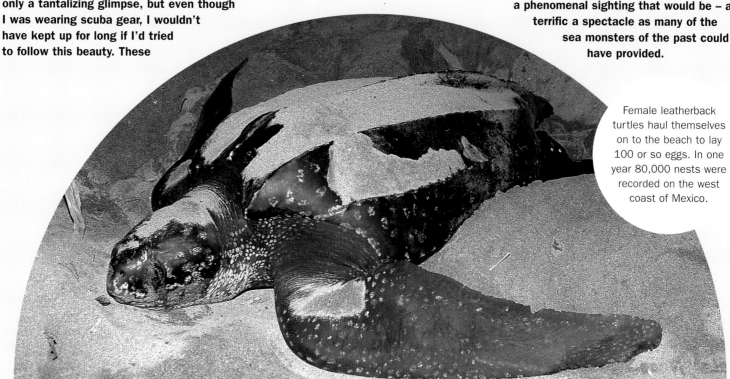

Female leatherback turtles haul themselves on to the beach to lay 100 or so eggs. In one year 80,000 nests were recorded on the west coast of Mexico.

Coelurosaur

The earliest meat-eating dinosaurs belonged to a group known as the coelurosaurs. Most were quite small and lived by scavenging and hunting anything that moved.

Name: Means 'hollow-tailed reptile'.
Type of animal: A primitive type of theropod (meat-eating) dinosaur.
When was it alive? The earliest coelurosaurs occur around 230–200 million years ago (Mid Triassic to Early Jurassic).

Pronunciation: See-LUR-oh-sawr.
Size: 2–3 metres (6–10 feet) in length.
Diet: They would generally hunt reptiles, insects, fish and other small animals.
Fossil finds: South America, North America, Europe, Australia and Africa.
Fact: The coelurosaurs are some of the most primitive of all the dinosaurs. It is from them that *Tyrannosaurus* and other giant meat-eaters are descended.

expect amphibians to have a soft, naked skin, but that's not the case with this grotesque creature – it has broad plates on its belly and bony outgrowths on its back. Spoilt for choice, with a mass of wriggling babies beneath it, the mastodonsaurus cocks its massive head – it measures 1.2 metres (4 feet) across the skull – before lunging downwards to clamp a wriggling nothosaur between its jaws.

The other babies slip away, flailing their flippers like clockwork toys, but now the whole world is against them. This time a cynodont, a land-based reptile the size of a small dog, sprints towards a couple of babies in the vanguard. It wrinkles the skin on its snout, which has the effect of twitching whisker-like hairs, which brush over the young nothosaurs. This is a final tactile check; now, satisfied that the prey is what it expects, the cynodont bites down on one of the nothosaurs and snaps it in two. Excited by the procession of food crawling in front of it, it twitches its tail and its body, with a thin covering of hair, shakes uncontrollably. It strikes again, plucking another nothosaur from the sand. The group to which cynodonts belong is the ancestor of the mammals that will one day dominate the earth, but reptiles don't have to worry just yet – for the next 150 million years no mammal bigger than a cat will emerge to challenge their superiority.

The baby nothosaurs still have to run the gauntlet of another meat-eater patrolling the water's edge. A 3-metre (10-foot) coelurosaur tackles one, biting out its throat. While the carnivore is occupied in bolting down its victim's flesh, the remaining nothosaurs make good their escape. Only half the babies will survive their desperate race across the beach.

The coelurosaur licks the fleck of blood from its lips. It's one of the first dinosaurs; the age of reptiles has just begun. For the next 165 million years, through the Triassic, Jurassic and Cretaceous periods, they will rule the Earth.

In the Triassic, primitive two-legged dinosaurs, like this coelophysis (a type of coelurosaur), began to appear all over the world.

155

million years ago

The Jurassic

The Jurassic sea is home to what some people believe is the largest predator of all time: liopleurodon. This marine reptile can grow to over 20 metres (65 feet) in length, has a superb sense of smell and ambushes from below. Not what you want underneath you when you go for a dip.

Deadly paradise

Close your eyes and think of England – more specifically, try to paint in your mind's eye a picture of the English countryside. A rolling expanse of hills, rivers, forests, lakes covered with grasses and deciduous trees such as oak, hazel and beech. The sea is icy cold, there are four clearly defined seasons and overall the weather is – well, it could be better. Picture yourself there: the chill wind on your skin, the smell of wet bark and grass, the sound of birdsong. Now get ready for a shock as we travel back 155 million years to the England of the Jurassic – the difference will blow you away.

The Europe of 155 million years ago is a completely unfamiliar world – flowers and grass, along with a whole host of plants we take for granted, are absent. Instead there is a spiky cornucopia of prehistoric flora such as conifers, ferns, column pines, cycads, bennetites and horsetails. The air doesn't dance with the twitter of birds, but is ripped up by the screech of pterosaurs with the occasional groan from a distant dinosaur. The climate is tropical, with seasons to match: a wet and a dry season instead of summer, autumn, winter and spring. In fact the climate on Earth is about as hot as it has ever got and the water here is a pleasant 20°C (70°F), as opposed to the 10°C (50°F) the twenty-first-century English are used to. But the most important difference of all is the sea level, which in the Jurassic is some 100 metres (330 feet) higher than it is today, so that vast tracts of Europe aren't land at all but seabed. With only the highest points above water, Jurassic Europe is not so much a landmass as a huge tableau of glittering islands set in a warm, shallow sea.

In fact, from above the water the England of 155 million years ago looks much like paradise, but beneath the waves lives such a fearsome

Hurricane Emilia over the Eastern Pacific Ocean, as seen from space. Massive storms like this were a common feature of the Jurassic.

YOU ARE HERE

The dinosaur *Eustreptospondylus* can be found on even the smallest of islands. When food runs short on one island, they simply swim to another.

The Jurassic at a glance

How bad? Second most dangerous sea.
How long ago? 155 million years.
Where? The sea around a group of islands in what will become southern England. The predators described here are common throughout a whole swathe of northern Europe.

Shape of the continents: During the Triassic the world was made up of one gargantuan supercontinent called Pangea, but by the Jurassic this is starting to break up into two massive continents called Laurasia and Gondwana.

What's new? This is the time when animals in North America and Europe reach their most extreme sizes, both on land and in the sea. As well as behemoths such as *Leedsichthys* and *Liopleurodon*, the Jurassic saw the rise of the most colossal dinosaurs of all: the sauropods.

THE HAZARDS

Top predator: *Liopleurodon*.
Other predators: *Metrioryhnchus*, *Hybodus* sharks.
Super-hurricanes: As in any tropical environment, there's a price to pay for the good weather – huge storms that feed off the energy stored in the water. Cyclones, hurricanes, typhoons, call them what you will, the most important thing to realize is that in the Jurassic they can be far more severe than even the worst of those seen today. From time to time, Jurassic storms are of such staggering brutality that they stir the ocean floor and kick up waves so enormous that whole islands are sluiced utterly clean of life.

On shore: How dangerous the shoreline is very much depends on where you are – the smaller islands cannot support huge predators, but there is still the odd dinosaur to contend with, including the 5-metre (16-foot) long *Eustreptospondylus*. On the mainland, there are considerably bigger creatures to worry about, like the *Allosaurus*, which is 12 metres (40 feet) long. Nothing that matches up to *Liopleurodon*, though.

Same place, different time –
two images of the English
countryside around Peterborough
in Cambridgeshire, separated by
155 million years.

collection of predators that you would have to
be virtually insane to get in the water here. This
is the second most dangerous sea of all time.

To understand what makes this environment tick
we need to start at the smaller end of the food chain.
This shallow sea is a fertile one, rich in nutrients and
capable of supporting life in abundance. Nutrients are washed
in off the land and, because the water is shallow, passing storms also
stir up organic matter from dead animals on the seabed. (And this
place sees some monumental storms.) It is the perfect environment
for plankton to thrive and at times the water gets so thick with these
teeming micro-organisms that the sharks can barely see past the end
of their noses. The plankton supports larger animals such as the
distinctive ammonites and the ubiquitous belemnites – squid-like
animals with a hard shell on the *inside* of their bodies.

All of this and the plentiful fish are food for the 'devil-horned'
shark, hybodus, and a whole array of sizeable marine reptiles:

Ammonites

When the first ammonites were discovered in England, they were commonly thought to be the remains of snakes that had been turned to stone. Science has since cleared up that little misunderstanding: far from being petrified reptiles, ammonites are members of the same class of molluscs as squid and octopus – the cephalopods.

As any ancient Greek will tell you, cephalopod means 'head-footed', a reference to the 'limbs' (or tentacles) that surround their mouth. Compared to other molluscs, such as clams, mussels or snails, most cephalopods are active hunters. However, ammonites weren't quite as dynamic in their lifestyle as squid or octopus; they are more often compared with *Nautilus*, another

Cretaceous ammonites had exotic shapes. Some bristled with spikes; others, like this *Euhoplites opalinus*, were covered with lumps and bumps.

cephalopod and the closest thing to an ammonite on the Earth today. Physically they are very similar, with their soft bodies inhabiting a gas-and-fluid-filled coiled shell which they use to control their buoyancy as they move up and down the water column. Like *Nautilus*, ammonites were not built for speed and didn't so much pursue their prey as bump into it – hence their diet of tiny crustaceans, single-celled organisms and, occasionally, much smaller ammonites.

The first ammonites with their fabulous coiled shells were on the scene far earlier than the Jurassic. Descended from straight-shelled molluscs called bactritids, they appeared as early as the Mid Devonian. (Their trademark shape most likely evolved because a compact coiled shell is more manoeuvrable in water than a long straight one.) It was the beginning of a very successful 290 million years on Earth. The ammonites made it through

The late-Cretaceous ammonite *Didymoceras stevensoni* is believed to have sat vertically in the water and spiralled up and down.

Although it might appear that the closest thing to an ammonite today is the *Nautilus*, they are in fact believed to be more closely related to squid.

some pretty severe extinctions and then, in the Jurassic, they really found their form, surging in numbers and diversifying into a huge variety of species: spiked ones, rippled ones, tiny ones, massive ones, some with the head floating upwards, others with the head pointing down.

Along with the dinosaurs and all the big marine reptiles, they disappeared completely at the end of the Cretaceous. One of the big mysteries is why something as diverse and numerous as the ammonites died out, while *Nautilus*, so similar in so many ways, made it through.

The classic spiral shape of a Jurassic ammonite. This fossil was found in Germany.

Ophthalmosaurus

A fast-moving ichthyosaur, ophthalmosaurus used its speed to catch fish and squid and to outrun its many enemies.

Name: Means 'eye reptile'.

Type of animal: A marine reptile, an ichthyosaur.

When was it alive? 165–150 million years ago (Jurassic).

Pronunciation: Off-THAL-moh-SAW-rus.

Size: Up to 5 metres (16 feet) in length.

Diet: Fish, ammonites and belemnites.

Fossil finds: Argentina, England and Germany.

Fact: Ophthalmosaurus had the largest eyes of any marine reptile.

The saucer-eyed ophthalmosaurus is one of the fastest creatures in the Jurassic – its main diet is squid-like animals called belemnites.

long-necked plesiosaurs such as cryptoclidus; the big-eyed ichthyosaur ophthalmosaurus; and the extraordinary metriorhynchus – over 4 metres (13 feet) long and a close relative of the crocodiles but totally adapted to an ocean-going lifestyle. Metrioryhnchus is descended from a forerunner of the crocodiles – one which looks much like the freshwater crocodiles of the twenty-first century – but the course of evolution has substantially modified the body of metriorhynchus for a marine existence. The feet have become flippers and the heavy armoured scutes of freshwater crocodilians have been lost in favour of sleek skin, for speed in the water. And there's not much croc-ness about the tail, either – it has developed a fluke much like that of a shark, great for bursts of speed. But metrioryhnchus still retains some close similarities to its freshwater relatives: a lethal set of teeth and the crocodilian trait of eating everything and anything that it can – fish, belemnites, ammonites and even the occasional pterosaur as it swoops down to catch fish. They are more particular about where they live – they like warm, salty water and tend to favour the shallower areas no more than a couple of days' swim from land. So as far as the metriorhynchus are concerned, the warm, shallow waters around the islands of what will become England are just about perfect.

And then there are the big fish – not just quite big, *really* big. In fact the biggest fish ever, leedsichthys – one that can grow up to a whopping 27 metres (nearly 90 feet) long – is found here. Compare that to the largest fish in twenty-first-century waters, the whale shark, which in the rarest cases can reach 20 metres (65 feet) in length. Like whale sharks,

Metriorhynchus

Metriorhynchus was an ancient relative of the crocodile that spent almost its entire life at sea. As well as hunting fish, it also liked to hide just under the water and grab passing pterosaurs.

Name: Means 'moderate snout'.

Type of animal: A marine crocodilian, a distant cousin to living crocodiles.

When was it alive? 160–150 million years ago (Mid Jurassic).

Pronunciation: MET-ri-oh-RINK-us.

Size: 3 metres (10 feet) in length.

Diet: Ammonites, belemnites, large fish, pterosaurs and anything else it was capable of catching.

Fossil finds: England, France, Chile and Argentina.

Fact: This snappy hunter could grab pterosaurs in mid-flight.

Nigel keeps trouble at bay – metriorhynchus need to be treated with as much respect as their relatives, the freshwater crocodiles.

Leedsichthys

Fish do not come any larger than
Leedsichthys, but this was a gentle
giant that lived by filtering small fish and
shrimps from the sea. Unfortunately its
size could not protect it from attack by
other predators.

Name: Means 'Leeds's fish', after Alfred
Leeds, a nineteenth-century English geologist.

Type of animal: A ray-finned fish, which means
that it is in the same general group as most
modern fish.

When was it alive? 165–155 million years ago
(Late Jurassic).

Pronunciation: Leeds-ICK-thees.

Size: Up to 27 metres (nearly 90 feet) in
length.

Diet: Small shrimps, jellyfish, small fish.

Fossil finds: England, France and Chile.

Fact: *Leedsichthys* had over 40,000
teeth which were used to sieve
small animals from the water.
It is probably the largest fish
ever to have lived.

leedsichthys are gentle giants, no danger to anything much larger than plankton, which they sieve out through an arrangement of 40,000 superfine teeth arranged in rows in front of their gills. At certain times of year, when the water goes milky with an explosion of plankton, they cruise open-mouthed through these islands in great shoals, like underwater zeppelins. Anyone who has swum with a whale shark will testify that it is an awesome experience. But then they haven't been in the Jurassic among a whole shoal of leedsichthys.

You'd have thought that a fish of this size would have little to fear from other animals, but there are at least two predators native to this area that will attack a full-grown leedsichthys. The first one is, somewhat surprisingly, metriorhynchus. In keeping with its opportunistic style of hunting, it has been known to take bites out of live leedsichthys. And as if being eaten alive wasn't bad enough, the second threat facing these huge creatures is a more terrifying beast altogether: again a reptile, but one that is almost as large as leedsichthys. Arguably the largest predator, on land or in the sea, of all time: liopleurodon.

Sometimes size is no protection – a dying leedsichthys can do little to save itself from being eaten alive, as both hybodus sharks and metriorhynchus take advantage of its weakened state.

Liopleurodon – the biggest predator ever?

That something far, far bigger than cryptoclidus, ophthalmosaurus or metriorhynchus hunts in these waters is obvious from the occasional partial skeleton on the seabed: here and there a complete tail, without a single bone from the rest of the body; elsewhere a head and forelimbs, with no trace of the tail. These are the remains of animals as much as 6 metres (20 feet) long that have been quite literally bitten in half.

Only a few times in its history has Earth witnessed a predator anything like the size of the culprit. Large male liopleurodon can reach 21 metres (70 feet) long, and there are thought to be a few exceptional individuals out there that touch 25 metres (80 feet). No one knows for sure, but teeth marks have been found in the bones of prey that can only have been made by a pliosaur of that size ('pliosaur' is the name given to short-necked plesiosaurs like liopleurodon). This is double the length of the largest land predator of all time, the dinosaur giganotosaurus, which measures a meagre 12 metres (40 feet) from head to tail. In the sea, though, animals can grow to be a whole lot bigger and there are one or two marine predators in the same size range as liopleurodon. Sperm whales over 21 metres (70 feet) long have been found (and who knows what we haven't found?), and in the Triassic some ichthyosaurs knock on 25 metres (80 feet). But while sperm whales and ichthyosaurs prey on things like squid, liopleurodon is equipped to kill much larger animals, making it a meaner monster all round.

The head alone is over 3 metres (10 feet) long and home to a fearsome collection of dagger-like teeth, the longest of which are at the tip of the snout. Eyes on top of its head reveal that liopleurodon attacks from below, while its chest shows an animal engineered for explosive ambush. A reinforced ribcage harbours colossal muscle structures designed to pull the flippers down in immensely powerful strokes as it launches itself unseen from the depths.

As with any marine hunter, catching prey is not the whole problem – a predator also has to be able to remove chunks of flesh, something that is far harder to do in water than on land. (Think apple-bobbing, but replace the apple with a 6-metre (20-foot) long reptile in its death throes.) Sharks have solved this problem by having such incredibly sharp teeth that the bite is normally sufficient to remove each mouthful, while crocodiles spin in the water to tear off bits of meat. Liopleurodon meanwhile has the thickest of

Liopleurodon

The largest predator of all time, *Liopleurodon* was capable of attacking and eating most animals in the ocean. As an air-breathing marine reptile it stayed close to the surface and would probably have fed on other marine reptiles such as the ichthyosaurs.

Name: Means 'smooth-sided tooth'.
Type of animal: A marine reptile; short-necked plesiosaur.
When was it alive? 160–155 million years ago (Mid to Late Jurassic).
Pronunciation: LIE-PLOO-ro-don.

Size: Up to 25 metres (80 feet) long.
Diet: Other marine reptiles, large fish, belemnites – almost anything it could catch and swallow.
Fossil finds: England, Germany and possibly Mexico.
Fact: *Liopleurodon*'s teeth were twice as long as those of *Tyrannosaurus*.

Dos and don'ts of Jurassic diving

Obviously the Jurassic wouldn't be the safest place to go diving, but if you were to try your luck there, you would need to follow some important guidelines:

● Avoid areas with bad visibility.

● *Liopleurodon* has such sensitive nostrils that you should never, ever go in the water with an open wound. To reduce your smell, cover yourself in petroleum jelly and, whatever you do, don't urinate in your wet suit.

● If possible, dive from a big boat. *Liopleurodon* hunts by ambushing from below and the silhouette of a small boat looks dangerously like an *Ophthalmosaurus* at the surface. If you have to use a small boat, be sure to have the outboard engine on at all times – the noise will lessen the chance of an attack. Never use the oars – they could be mistaken for the flippers of *Liopleurodon*'s prey.

● The best protection is a 'smell suit' (see opposite). This is a wet suit modified to secrete chemicals that *Liopleurodon* finds objectionable. The smell of rotting reptile flesh is particularly effective.

Too close for comfort

This is what a *Liopleurodon*'s favourite prey, *Ophthalmosaurus*, looks like from below.

And this is how your boat will look – in murky water, a *Liopleurodon* could easily mistake a small boat for prey.

necks, allowing it to thrash its head from side to side and rip its prey apart.

Reptiles, as a rule, cannot smell underwater – when crocodiles or turtles dive, they close off their nostrils completely to prevent water getting in. But liopleurodon, along with all the plesiosaurs, has an arrangement that is utterly different and is the key to its success as a hunter (see box below). Its unique sensory system allows a liopleurodon to detect minute amounts of chemicals in the water – traces of blood, excrement, an

Water out

Water in

Even when closed, a *Liopleurodon*'s mouth is far from watertight and so as it swims forward, water is forced in. Grooves in the top of the palate then guide the water into two nostril openings in the roof of the mouth and up through S-shaped tubes leading to the external nostrils on top of the snout. Only sharks have anything remotely similar.

Using a smell suit

In the Second World War, the US Navy used life jackets impregnated with a chemical similar to that found in decomposing shark meat. This unusual feature was designed to protect pilots downed over water from shark attacks – sharks will not eat a carcass if it is rotting. The same is true of *Liopleurodon*. A human being would barely be classed as a light snack for an adult *Liopleurodon* – nonetheless, if you did plan to dive with one, a way of making the whole experience safer would be to build your own smell suit, a device which protects the wearer by taking advantage of the pliosaurs' highly developed sense of smell (see box below). The suit is covered in a network of fine pipes dotted with holes, connected to a small bottle containing a chemical called putrescene – an extract of rotting reptile flesh.

In the event of a *Liopleurodon* getting too close, the putrescene can be pumped through the pipes, creating a cloud of the chemical around the diver. In theory this should make the diver extremely unappetizing. As well as detering predators who are not attracted to rotting meat, in most animals the smell of death (especially of their own kind) is associated with danger and therefore acts as a warning, telling them to keep away.

The massive eyes of the fast-moving ophthalmosaurus enable it to hunt in low light conditions, like murky water and at dusk.

animal giving birth – but, most crucially of all, it can tell where these smells are coming from. Liopleurodon smells in the same way that human beings hear: our brain figures out where a sound is coming from through the difference in the sound reaching the right and left ears. For liopleurodon, it is the smallest difference in the smell reaching its left nostril and its right that signals a scent's origin and allows it to sniff out its prey before it runs any risk of being seen.

Survival

We've talked about liopleurodon's prowess as a hunter, but life is all about balance. Just as predators evolve into more sophisticated killers, so prey evolve into more difficult targets and the creatures that share these waters with liopleurodon have all manner of strategies to keep themselves out of the jaws of death.

For leedsichthys, their size is their protection. A healthy adult is by and large too much trouble for a liopleurodon to take on. But sick or injured individuals, particularly those that have become separated from the shoal, are vulnerable to attack.

For the smaller marine animals, survival comes down to three things: senses, speed and spikes. Ophthalmosaurus' most distinctive feature, and one critical for its survival, is its huge eyes, which are capable of seeing in the gloomiest of conditions. There is an obvious two-fold advantage for the animal – it can pick out its prey and it can outsee its predators. Ophthalmosaurus' superlative eyesight allows it to hunt squid and belemnites at night, when it is safest from a liopleurodon attack. Though smell is important to liopleurodon in finding its victims, it relies heavily on sight to

Plesiosaurs

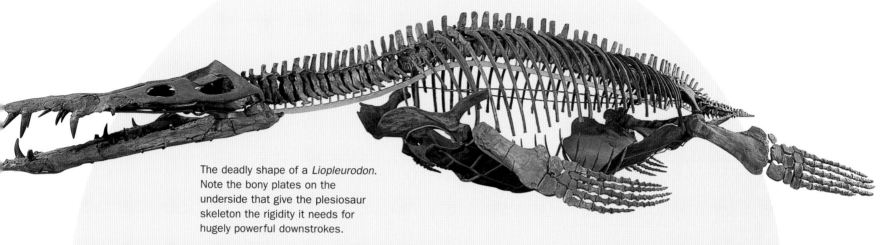

The deadly shape of a *Liopleurodon*.
Note the bony plates on the
underside that give the plesiosaur
skeleton the rigidity it needs for
hugely powerful downstrokes.

Plesiosaurs are unique. With that elongated body with its two pairs of paddle-like flippers, there is nothing else quite like them – never has been, never will be. In fact, they are a defining feature of the Mesozoic oceans.

The name plesiosaur means 'almost lizards', a reference to their body shape, which does have a little bit of lizardness about it – certainly more so than other marine reptiles such as the ichthyosaurs, which no longer look anything like the land-based reptiles from which they evolved. Plesiosaurs derive from nothosaurs (see Chapter 3); the big change is in the limbs, which have gone from webbed feet to those big, broad flippers. They use the flippers like wings, alternating the back and front pairs in powerful down-strokes – literally flying through the water, much as a turtle does. Aside from having to return to the surface to breathe, these are creatures entirely attuned to life in the sea.

The success of this design is mirrored in the great variety of plesiosaurs which appeared from the early Jurassic onwards. They fall into two main groups: short-necked and long-necked. *Cryptoclidus* is an example of a long-necked plesiosaur. Its delicate skull and fine teeth (almost a hundred in total) were suited for small, soft prey such as fish. The unusually long neck was probably an adaptation for hunting in the sediment-rich waters of northern Europe – as *Cryptoclidus* moved towards a shoal of fish in murky water, at first only its tiny head would be visible. Only when it was too late would the prey become aware of the huge, fish-devouring reptile to which the head belonged.

Short-necked plesiosaurs (or pliosaurs) such as *Liopleurodon* were very different beasts: far more compact, with deeper bodies and thicker, stronger necks attached to long, slender jaws. Their teeth were by and large stouter and capable of locking on to more robust prey – such as, for instance, *Cryptoclidus*.

A medium-sized plesiosaur, cryptoclidus had long, fine teeth designed to catch slippery prey like fish and squid. They are one of the least dangerous predators around at this time but, at up to 8 metres (26 feet) long, you'd still get quite a shock if you bumped into one.

Hybodus

The devilish-looking *Hybodus* was a true shark and would have hunted and swum in a similar way to most modern small sharks. The spine on its dorsal fin would have deterred predators from trying to attack it.

Name: No one seems to know how *Hybodus* got its name.

Type of animal: A shark.

When was it alive? 230–90 million years ago (Triassic to Cretaceous).

Pronunciation: Hie-BOW-dus.

Size: 2 metres (6 feet 6 inches) in length.

Diet: Fish, shellfish, belemnites and other sharks.

Fossil finds: Asia, Europe, Africa and North America.

Fact: The spine on *Hybodus'* back would have got stuck in the mouth of any potential predator, making it impossible to swallow.

make the kill; like other marine ambush predators such as the great white shark, it spots its victims by looking out for silhouettes at the surface. At night there are no silhouettes.

Other senses play a big part in cryptoclidus' self-preservation. Being a plesiosaur, cryptoclidus boasts the same ability to smell underwater as liopleurodon does, together with a sense of hearing completely adapted to the marine environment: unlike those of its land ancestors, cryptoclidus' earbones are fused together. This arrangement might make cryptoclidus virtually deaf above the water but, due to the way sound waves travel through water, it is remarkably attuned to sounds beneath it. Such a specialized sense is as useful in finding something to eat as it is in avoiding being eaten.

When it comes to speed, it is ophthalmosaurus that has the upper hand over virtually every other animal around. Although unrelated, it shares a similar body shape with the speed merchants of the twenty-first-century seas, namely dolphins and tuna. The rounded body, smooth skin and deep, powerful tail allow ophthalmosaurus to reach speeds in excess of 40 kilometres (25 miles) per hour and outpace any liopleurodon – provided it sees it in time.

Hybodus, of course, has all of these protective mechanisms and more. Like most sharks, it is fast and has superbly developed senses: smell, hearing and sight, together with the ability to detect the electromagnetic signals given off by the muscles of other animals. These all serve to protect it as well as making it an effective predator. But the spikes alongside the dorsal fin are plainly not for hunting. These very same spikes are seen on much smaller twenty-first-century relatives such as the Port Jackson shark and the Mexican hornshark, where one of their functions is to stick in the throat of any animal that tries to eat them. If a liopleurodon does manage to catch a hybodus, it'll probably regurgitate it.

Some modern sharks, like this Mexican hornshark, photographed off Baja in Mexico, retain the same spiky defences as the Jurassic hybodus, although they are nothing like as large.

75

million years ago

The Cretaceous

What makes this sea worse than any other is that there isn't just one predator to worry about, there's a whole blood-curdling collection of them – sharks, lightning-fast killer fish, such as xiphactinus (pictured), and fearsome marine reptiles called mosasaurs. Scariest of them all are the snake-like giant mosasaurs.

Don't go in the water!

Given the other oceans covered in this book, the claim that this is the most dangerous of them all is not one we make lightly. What can be worse than a sea terrorized by a giant killer fish like megalodon or dunkloesteus, or a monster reptile like liopleurodon? Answer: a sea which has giant killer fish *and* monster reptiles in abundance. Unlike all the other seas in this book, the main danger in the Cretaceous waters doesn't come from the direction of one heavyweight predator. It comes from every direction, courtesy of the meanest collection of predators nature has ever assembled under water. Welcome to Hell's Aquarium.

One of the best places to experience the full horror of Cretaceous marine life is Kansas. This may strike you as a little strange given that in the twenty-first century this huge, flat area of land is about as

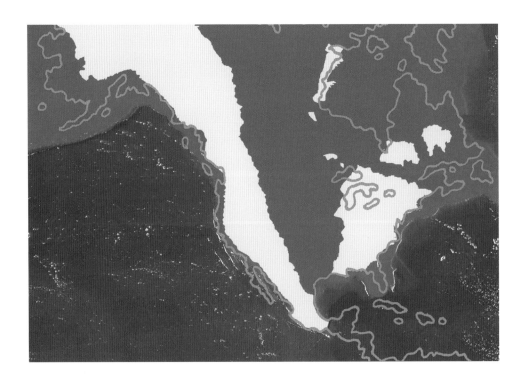

This map shows the inland sea that covered much of North America during the Cretaceous. Called the Western Interior Seaway, at some points it extended all the way up to the Arctic Circle.

Tyrannosaurus rex first appeared on the scene about 75 million years ago. It was the beginning of the end for dinosaurs.

YOU ARE HERE

The Cretaceous at a glance

How bad? The most dangerous sea of all.

How long ago? 75 million years.

Where? Inland sea over Kansas, but in fact many of the predators are widespread throughout the world's oceans.

Shape of the continents: The Earth is starting to look a lot more recognizable, as the continents continue to break up. Africa has moved away from South America and is now heading up towards Europe, India is on a collision course with Asia, while the Atlantic Ocean has been formed as North America and Europe drift further apart.

What's new? Since their appearance in the Late Jurassic, flowering plants have gone from strength to strength and have now become dominant, elbowing the ferns and cycads to one side. This has allowed a partnership to blossom between the insects and the flowers – the first pollinating insects appear at this time. Snakes are another new addition to the world (surprisingly, they're a lot less ancient than other reptiles such as crocodiles, lizards, dinosaurs and turtles). On the dinosaur side of things the Cretaceous represents a time of enormous diversity.

THE HAZARDS

Top predator: Giant mosasaurs (*Hainosaurus* is thought to be the biggest species). These would be frightening enough on their own, but they travel in groups. (There is no collective term for them, but we suggest that a 'murder of mosasaurs' would be about right.)

Other predators: *Xiphactinus*, smaller mosasaurs, a variety of sharks including *Squalicorax*, giant squid, smaller pliosaurs such as *Dolichorynchops*.

On shore: If the *Tyrannosaurus rex* doesn't get you, the raptors will – *Dromaeosaurus* (close relatives of the *Velociraptor*) attack in packs and have scythe-like claws designed for disembowelling their prey.

Tyrannosaurus

A giant meat-eating dinosaur built to hunt and destroy other large dinosaurs. Like other dinosaurs it perished during the extinction event of 65 million years ago.

Name: *Tyrannosaurus* meaning 'terrible reptile', *rex* meaning 'king', because when it was found it was the largest known meat-eating dinosaur.

Type of animal: A theropod dinosaur.

When was it alive? 75–65 million years ago (Late Cretaceous).

Pronunciation: Tye-RAN-uh-SAW-rus.

Size: 12 metres (40 feet) in length.

Diet: A serious meat-eater, hunting other dinosaurs, reptiles and mammals.

Fossil finds: North America.

Fact: Even though *Tyrannosaurus* is no longer the largest meat-eating dinosaur (at least three others are known to have been bigger), it is still the most famous dinosaur of all time.

far away from the sea as you can get in the USA. When most people think of Kansas they think of farming, tornadoes and, of course, *The Wizard of Oz*. But over the last couple of centuries the earth here has given up far more than crops – fossil after fossil of marine predators has revealed that Kansas should also be famous for its watery past; a past when the central part of the USA was completely submerged under an inland sea and most of Kansas was seabed. That's where we need to go now, so click those magic heels and say, 'There's no place like the Cretaceous, there's no place like the Cretaceous, there's no place like the Cretaceous, there's no place like the Cretaceous …'

So here we are, in the late Cretaceous, standing on a rocky shoreline in the very east of Kansas. To the west is the glittering expanse of the inland sea. Given that these are the most hazardous waters of all, it's probably best not to plunge right in – let's get a feel for where we are first.

The Cretaceous is the last of the three great ages of dinosaurs. To put it in a nutshell, dinosaurs appeared in the Triassic, grew to enormous sizes in the Jurassic and then spent the Cretaceous diversifying into any number of forms before their demise (due in about 10 million years' time). North America is a good place to find some of the best-known of them: the duckbills, the raptors, the armoured ankylosaurs and good old tyrannosaurus rex. It's quite possible to see any one of these wandering down the beach, but at certain times of year a far more likely sight is a gathering of big ugly birds.

Around the coasts of North America, including this inland sea, huge colonies of a seabird called hesperornis congregate to mate. The sound, sight (and smell) are beyond belief, and if you think you've seen a colony of seabirds before, now's the time to think again. Hesperornis are nearly 2 metres (6 feet 6 inches) long and have teeth.

They are so large that they can't even walk; instead, they slide along the rocky beaches on their bellies. The fact that they are so completely unsuited to getting around on land is something that they have to live with for the duration of the breeding season. At least they're comparatively safe up on the beach. There may be the odd tyrannosaurus rex or raptor to worry

Hesperornis

One of the so-called 'toothed birds' commonly found in the Cretaceous of North America and elsewhere. Flightless and unable to walk properly, *Hesperornis* spent most of its time at sea hunting fish and squid, coming on land to mate and lay eggs.

Name: Means 'western bird', because its remains were first found in the USA.

Type of animal: A 'toothed bird'.

When was it alive? 80–65 million years ago (Late Cretaceous).

Pronunciation: HES-per-OR-nis.

Size: 2 metres (6 feet 6 inches) in length.

Diet: A marine predator eating fish, ammonites and belemnites.

Fossil finds: North America.

Fact: While birds might be famous for having tiny brains, the brains of *Hesperornis* were small even by bird standards.

Hesperornis gather on the beach to breed – a noisy and smelly spectacle that is repeated along much of the inland sea shoreline.

An illustration of the skull of *Hesperornis* showing its numerous teeth – 28 in the upper jaw, 66 in the lower.

Hens' teeth

As the expression 'rare as hens' teeth' testifies, birds these days don't have teeth. However, as fossils of *Hesperornis* reveal, they used to.

When the first examples were found, their significance was missed. The famous American palaeontologist Othniel Marsh looked at them and, since he wasn't expecting a bird to have teeth, thought the fossil must be a composite of two animals. (Marsh was the arch-rival of E. D. Cope, the palaeontologist infamous for putting the head of *Elasmosaurus* on the wrong end of its body – see The big blunder, page 118. Marsh and Cope had one of the most vitriolic and drawn-out arguments in the history of science.) When it was realized that the remains belonged to just one animal, and that it was indeed a bird with teeth extremely similar to those in reptiles, there was a huge stir in the scientific community. This was evidence for birds being descended from reptiles and, as scientists now widely believe, from dinosaurs. It was also cited in support of Darwin's theory of evolution.

about, but the rest of the year they spend at sea, paddling along above some *real* killers.

Hesperornis, so useless on the shore, are built for diving, and as soon as they hit the water these birds turn from cumbersome crawlers to superb swimmers. With strong rhythmic kicks their oversized feet power them head first towards the swirling shoals of fish around the rocky shoreline. Most birds have light, hollow bones to help them fly, but not hesperornis. Like penguins in the twenty-first century, they have thickened bones to make their bodies heavier, which helps them to dive and means that they have to use less energy to overcome their buoyancy.

Mean as they look, hesperornis are fairly low down the food chain. As they hunt these fish-laden waters, they are constantly running a lethal gauntlet. To find out why, we need to dip our toes in the water and meet the creatures that give the Cretaceous such a bad name.

Shallow death

We have said that what makes this sea dangerous is the sheer range of large marine predators around. There is, however, a recurring theme among them – many of them belong to a group of snake-like hunters called mosasaurs. These formidable marine reptiles come in all manner of size and form, but without doubt they represent the ruling class in the Cretaceous predator game.

Close to shore where we're starting are some of the smaller mosasaurs (though when we say 'smaller', it's all relative). They have

A 4-metre (13-foot) long halisaurus loiters in an underwater cave. They can hold their breath for over an hour, while waiting to ambush prey above them.

Halisaurus

Thought to be closely related to snakes, mosasaurs had extremely long tails (up to half their body length) and swallowed their prey whole. Widespread throughout the world, they diversified into an amazing variety of species, from small coastal dwellers like *Halisaurus* to monstrous open-water predators.

Name: Means 'sea lizard'.

Type of animal: A mosasaur – a now extinct group of marine reptiles.

When was it alive? 86–65 million years ago (Late Cretaceous).

Pronunciation: HAL-i-SAWR-uhs.

Size: 3–4 metres (10–13 feet) in length.

Diet: Fish, molluscs and seabirds.

Fossil finds: North America, South America, North Africa and Europe.

Fact: The first mosasaur fossils were discovered around 1780, almost 50 years before the first dinosaur fossils.

thick-set, eel-like bodies and all the cuddliness of a snake crossed with a shark. These are menacing-looking creatures. Some, it has to be said, aren't as bad as they appear. For instance, you'd be pretty safe if you came face to face with the 7.5-metre (25-foot) long fat-headed globidens. This has a mouthful of flat teeth designed for crushing molluscs. It is one of the more specialized mosasaurs and one of the few that doesn't take large prey. But the problem the hesperornis have – as indeed you would have if you were to dive here – is that most of the mosasaurs *are* as bad as they appear.

Loitering in the submarine caves and cracks under the hesperornis ledges are halisaurus. Some 4 metres (13 feet) in length, their dentition is a lot more typical of mosasaurs than of globidens. Powerful jaws sport a set of short, sharp teeth designed to grab prey and hold on to the victim during its death throes. When the hesperornis leave their rocky ledges to dive for fish, the halisaurus are down below, watching and waiting for an opportunity to get their mouth round a nice bit of bird flesh. The flash of a tail, a cloud of blood in the water, another victim. On this coast, not many hesperornis live long enough to die of old age.

Mosasaur teeth might be great for piercing the skin of their prey, but they are less suitable for slicing flesh, so once a halisaurus has caught its prey, it proceeds to swallow it. Its jaw has flexible joints within it and can open incredibly wide. Bit by bit, it ratchets the hapless prey down into its throat. Extra teeth (called pterygoid teeth) on the roof of its mouth help this grim process along: they grip on to the body to keep it in position while the jaw moves forward. Mosasaurs, like snakes, eat their prey whole.

Then, of course, you've got the sharks to worry about. There is nothing here as large as megalodon – which won't appear for another 60 million years (see Chapter 7) – nonetheless a full range

The snake connection

Mosasaurs are distantly related to the monitor lizards such as Komodo dragons, but their fossils speak of an even closer kinship with snakes. The skulls are amazingly similar, with a virtually identical configuration of bones. Most revealing is the jaw mechanism, which in both types of animal is engineered to allow large prey to be swallowed whole. In snakes the jaw is especially pliable – the jawbones are not even connected by ligament. And then there are the double rows of pterygoid teeth in the roof of the mouth, which are present in all mosasaurs and snakes.

Some argue that this is just a case of 'parallel' evolution – that both types of animal have independently evolved the same solution to the problem of trying to manipulate prey into the stomach without having effective limbs for the job. But it is more likely that snakes and mosasaurs shared a common ancestor millions of years earlier – perhaps a

A skull of the mosasaur *Platecarpus*, found in western Kansas – at the rear of the roof of the mouth the characteristic double row of pterygoid teeth is clearly visible.

Down in one – a scrub python that has swallowed a wallaby. Eating their prey whole is a trait shared by both snakes and mosasaurs.

smallish reptile whose forebears had left the land and adapted to life in the sea. Another implication of this is that the first snakes, descended from this common ancestor, didn't live on land at all but were sea animals whose descendants eventually came on to land, probably in the late Cretaceous.

of good-sized sharks such as squalicorax (aka the 'crow shark') regard hesperornis as fair game, and would have the same view of a human being if they were to see one. Oh, and we nearly forgot to mention the giant squid, which are between 8 and 9 metres (25 and 30 feet) long. Unlike the giant squid of the twenty-first century, which are never a problem for man because they like cold, extremely deep waters, these squid are shallow, warm-sea dwellers. Get in a tangle with one of these and you will definitely end up sleeping with the fishes.

Well, that's the small dangers dealt with. In the twenty-first century they'd probably be the top predators, but here in the Cretaceous they are merely some of the less substantial (though frequent) causes of death – the lieutenants of the food chain, if you like. To meet what we might call the generals and indeed the supreme commander we have to head further out into the open sea, where deeper water harbours more profound perils: ever larger mosasaurs and a vicious, fast-moving fish called xiphactinus.

An ROV (remote operated vehicle) is definitely the safest and most sensible way to get close to the sea creatures of the Cretaceous.

Where angels fear to swim

Deeper water also provides a great opportunity to spot some of the other marvels of Cretaceous marine life. In a world where predators are so large, some prey species have themselves grown massive as a form of defence. Elasmosaurus is one startling example – it is one of the last species of plesiosaur and arguably the most amazing-looking sea monster ever (when nineteenth-century palaeontologists first look at its bones they think they've found a sea dragon). From tip of head to tip of tail it is 15 metres (50 feet) and it has the most

Dos and don'ts of Cretaceous diving

Given the range of different predators here, no one precaution would be effective against all the perils on offer in the waters of the Cretaceous. Anything that works against the predominant marine reptiles – the mosasaurs – would be unlikely to protect against fish predators like *Xiphactinus* and *Squalicorax*, or for that matter giant squid. Of all the options – chemical deterrents, electrical fields, chain mail, electric prods, etc. – a cage would provide the widest protection, as long as care was taken to restrict the holes in the cage to stop smaller mosasaurs gaining access.

But it has to be said that if you wanted to get a very close look at these animals the safest method would be to get a piece of machinery to do it for you. Remote operated vehicles (ROV) are normally used by commercial diving outfits to do work or inspections at depths where it is preferable not to send divers. An ROV is equipped with an onboard camera, which would allow an operator on a boat to have a good look around the Cretaceous ocean without getting their feet wet (or bitten off).

Elasmosaurus

The largest of the long-necked plesiosaurs, *Elasmosaurus* spent its days swimming slowly near the surface, using its long neck to sneak up on unsuspecting shoals of fish.

Name: Means 'thin-plated reptile', because of the plate-like nature of some of its bones.

Type of animal: A plesiosaur, a now-extinct group of marine reptiles.

When was it alive? 85–65 million years ago (Late Cretaceous).

Pronunciation: Eh-LAZZ-mo-SAWR-us.

Size: 15 metres (50 feet) in length, most of it neck.

Diet: Small fish, ammonites, belemnites, etc.

Fossil finds: USA, Russia and Japan.

Facts: The average *Elasmosaurus* had more than 10 kilograms (22 pounds) in its stomach. In its neck it had 74 vertebrae – humans have just seven.

The big blunder

It is all too easy to mock the mistakes people made early on in palaeontology. With the benefit of hindsight some of the theories and reconstructions that resulted from early discoveries appear absurd to us today, but of course those scientists *didn't* have the benefit of hindsight. Having said that, a little bit of mockery can't hurt, so we hope you don't mind us indulging ourselves just this once.

One of the most embarrassing errors in palaeontology was made in 1869 when the famous Edward Drinker Cope, a towering figure in scientific circles at the time, reconstructed an *Elasmosaurus* with the head on the wrong end. Plainly, a fairly major error.

The fossils had been discovered in Kansas in 1868 by a military surgeon who sent the bones to Philadelphia for Cope to look at. In those days transport between Kansas and Philadelphia was rudimentary and the journey itself, a combination of

On his death, the controversial American palaeontologist Edward Drinker Cope donated his body to science, believing himself to be a perfect human specimen. Someone later stole his skull.

wagon train and railroad, would have resulted in the bones being fairly jumbled up before Cope eventually saw them. To make matters worse he apparently examined them in a bit of a hurry before publishing a drawing of the animal, named *Elasmosaurus platyurus*, in a paper.

It was Cope's colleague, Joseph Leidy, who dropped him in it – he noticed that Cope had not looked at the vertebrae properly and announced that Cope had got everything back to front. In a damage-limitation exercise Cope tried to withdraw all the incriminating drawings from circulation. But he was too late to stop publication and he wasn't able to get all the drawings back.

The paper was republished in 1870 with the head the right way around, but Cope struggled to live the episode down and things were just a little frosty between Cope and Leidy for a good while afterwards.

Cope's first reconstruction of *Elasmosaurus* looks convincing enough, but in fact the head is on the wrong end.

Cope's amended drawing correctly shows that this was an animal with a long neck and *not* a long tail.

118 THE CRETACEOUS

Archelon

The largest turtle ever to have lived, it would have spent most of its life at sea eating jellyfish and ammonites and occasionally grazing on seaweed. It would have returned to land only to mate and lay eggs.

Name: Means 'large turtle', because of its extreme size.

Type of animal: A large turtle, part of the extinct protostegid turtle group.

When was it alive? 75–65 million years ago (Late Cretaceous).

Pronunciation: ARK-eh-lon.

Size: 4.5 metres (15 feet) in length.

Diet: Jellyfish, ammonites and belemnites, plus some plants.

Fossil finds: North America.

Fact: *Archelon* may well have spent several months of the year sleeping on the seabed.

exaggerated shape of any plesiosaur. Many species that have gone before have had long necks, but elasmosaurus has taken things to a magnificent extreme. Over half of its body length is neck. But why on earth should any animal evolve such an extraordinary feature? Well, one reason is to give it the upper hand when hunting fish. Elasmosaurus preys on small fish, and in murky water, or at dusk, it has the advantage that the fish cannot see the huge body at the other end of its neck. All the fish see is a small head which doesn't look too threatening. By the time they realize there's a massive reptilian body attached, they're already inside it.

To help them deal with all this fish they catch, elasmosaurus, like other plesiosaurs, add a strange supplement to their diet – they eat stones. Inside the stomach of an elasmosaurus there may be as many as 600 stones, a few well over 1 kilogram (2¼ pounds) in weight. Called gastroliths, these help both to grind down food and to counteract the air in the animal's lungs, allowing it to stay neutrally buoyant. Due to the endless tumbling around inside the stomach the gastroliths get worn down and have to be replenished. Elasmosaurus travel huge distances and some even return to the same river mouth every year, literally to fill their faces with rock.

Another creature from the 'bigger is safer' school of survival is archelon, a turtle which is to other turtles what an aircraft carrier is to a

A man stands next to the skeleton of an archelon in the Yale Peabody Museum in America. The fossil was found in South Dakota, which lies to the north of Kansas, and would have been covered by the inland sea during periods of the Cretaceous.

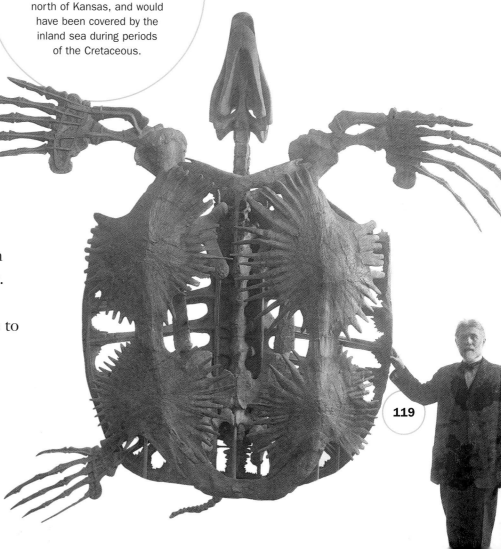

Nigel enjoys the ride of his life on an archelon. If you can stay on its back, you'll be out of the way of its beak, but you never know what may attack the archelon!

fishing boat. Archelon has a flipper span of up to 5.25 metres (18 feet), can weigh over 2 tonnes and has an awesomely powerful hooked beak, which could snap a diver's leg in two if one were stupid enough to annoy it. To get so big, evolution has made a compromise. Archelon does not have the hard enamel shell of smaller turtles, because on a creature of this size such a shell would become far too heavy. Instead, its carapace is made of tough skin stretched over a framework of thick bone (much like on a leatherback turtle). The underside is even tougher, consisting of a thick, reinforced lattice of bone. These defences are protection

enough against most of the predators, but tooth marks on the shell, missing flippers and the odd shattered skeleton on the seabed are testament to the fact that even archelon can fall prey here – especially to the giant mosasaurs.

Aside from mosasaurs and sharks, there is another hellish inhabitant of these waters which, if you're really lucky, can be seen launching out of the water and crashing down to rid itself of parasites: xiphactinus, a fish that can grow to 6–7 metres (20–23 feet) long, weighs up to a third of a tonne and is as ugly as sin. One look at it and it is plain to see how it gets its nickname, the 'bulldog fish'. The huge, square down-turned mouth is bristling with long, viciously sharp teeth and, like the mosasaurs', its jaws are designed to open extremely wide to accommodate prey much larger than it really ought to be able to tackle.

But xiphactinus' particular *forte* is high-speed attacks out of nowhere. Its body shape gives it away as an extremely fast animal: it is similar to that of other ocean speedsters like swordfish, tuna and tarpon – long, deep and sleek, going to an even deeper forked tail on a narrow base. No one has ever measured the top speed of a xiphactinus, but it must be near 60 kilometres (40 miles) per hour –

Xiphactinus

A streamlined and powerful fish that could swim at speed through the sea. Its mouth could open extremely wide, allowing it to swallow other large fish whole.

Name: Means 'swift swordfish', because of its broad resemblance to a modern swordfish.

Type of animal: An extinct type of fish.

When was it alive? 90–65 million years ago (Late Cretaceous).

Pronunciation: Zie-FAK-tin-us.

Size: 6 metres (20 feet) in length.

Diet: It was a pursuit hunter, chasing other large fish.

Fossil finds: North America.

Fact: *Xiphactinus* was a fast mover and could have jumped clear of the water as dolphins do today.

This famous 'fish within a fish' fossil was discovered by George Sternberg in 1952. It shows a xiphactinus with a fish measuring 2 metres (6 foot 6 inches) in length in its gut. Clearly this was its last meal and most likely what killed it.

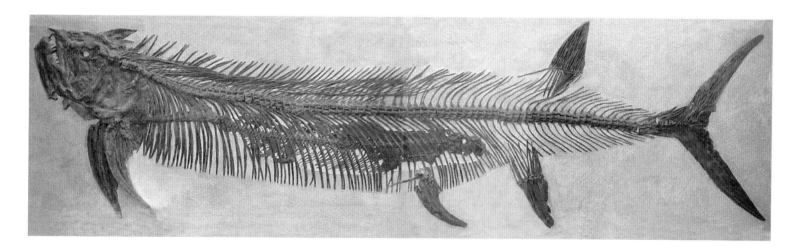

Giant mosasaurs

Towards the end of the Cretaceous, the giant mosasaurs were undoubtedly the top predators. The North American species *Tylosaurus* got towards 15 metres (50 feet) long, while the largest species known, *Hainosaurus*, reached 17 metres (56 feet).
Name: 'Mosa' is the Latin name for the Meuse River in Holland, near the underground limestone mine where their fossils were first

found, so 'mosasaur' is a 'Meuse lizard'; *Tylosaurus* means 'swollen lizard'; *Hainosaurus* 'Haine lizard', after the River Haine in Belgium, where fossils were discovered.
Type of animal: A mosasaur, a now extinct group of marine reptiles.
When was it alive? 89–65 million years ago (Late Cretaceous).
Pronunciation: TIE-low-SAWR-us, EN-o-SAWR-us.
Size: Up to 17 metres (56 feet) in length.
Diet: *Hesperornis*, sharks, large fish, turtles, ammonites, smaller mosasaurs and other large marine reptiles.
Fossil finds: North America, Europe.
Fact: Fossil evidence suggests that giant mosasaurs ate almost anything in their path, including other mosasaurs.

fast enough that you'd have little chance of seeing it coming, and even less chance of getting away if you did. In exceptionally clear water with visibility of 30 metres (100 feet) or so, if it came out of the deep at full speed it would still be visible for only two seconds before it hit you. A sobering thought and another very good reason not to get in the water here.

The main monster

Of course the biggest reason of all to stay on your boat is the presence of giant mosasaurs. (In fact they are widespread: Europe, Africa, even New Zealand all have their fair share of these monstrous reptiles.) There is something about the mosasaur design that has allowed them to diversify into species of all sizes, going from the reasonably small right up to giants like hainosaurus, which are unreasonably large. These are very much the top predators of their time – hainosaurus is the marine equivalent of tyrannosaurus rex, but a good deal bigger.

Most things that are true for coastal mosasaurs are true for ocean-going giant mosasaurs like hainosaurus, only on a larger scale. They have the same long, snake-like bodies, expanding jaws and a habit of eating other animals whole. It is their size that is so off the scale – 15–17 metres (50–55 feet) long. At that size just about everything else in the water is on their menu – including 6-metre (20-foot) long sharks, turtles and even other species of mosasaur. Then, of course, there are the animals at the surface of the water like the hesperornis and low-swooping pteranodon – tasty snacks to a giant mosasaur. Hainosaurus in particular is not a fussy eater, but will attack just about anything.

The huge wingspan of pteranodon enables them to glide huge distances in search of fish, their main diet.

Pteranodon

A graceful giant, gliding low across the sea's surface looking for fish. The large crest on its head was found only on males and may have been used during mating.

Name: Means 'toothless wing'.

Type of animal: A pterosaur, a type of extinct flying reptile.

When was it alive? 120–65 million years ago (Early to Late Cretaceous).

Pronunciation: Teh-RAN-o-DON.

Size: 8-metre (26-foot) wingspan.

Diet: It would hunt fish on the wing.

Fossil finds: North America, South America, Europe and Asia.

Fact: Despite its enormous wingspan, *Pteranodon*'s hollow bones and incredibly thin crust meant its weight was only one sixth of a man's.

Unlike xiphactinus, giant mosasaurs are not capable of sustained periods of speed and rely on short bursts of power to ambush their prey, usually at the surface. (This is how most mosasaurs hunt, although there are exceptions: platecarpus dives deep to feed, but since it has to return to the surface rapidly to breathe afterwards, it often suffers from the bends.) Just imagine a full-sized mosasaur on an attack run, an evil-looking reptile the weight of a truck barrelling up from the depths, totally focused on its victim. A bone-crunching impact, bodies breaking the surface and then a struggle before the prey is weak enough to be worked into the mosasaur's stomach. Mosasaurs frequently lose teeth in these devastating attacks, but as with sharks these are constantly replaced so that the predator always has a mouthful of sharp fangs.

But while giant mosasaurs can be said to rule this sea, even they have reason to fear it. Some marine reptiles, such as turtles, return to the beach to lay eggs, but the mosasaurs give birth to live young out in open water. A female may have three or four offspring which, from the moment of their birth, are sitting ducks for the large predators that give this sea its fearful reputation. To give their young some measure of protection, giant mosasaurs often swim together in groups. So as if encountering one wasn't bad enough, you're more likely to bump into a whole crowd of them …

A pteranodon looking for fish comes to a grizzly end in the mouth of a giant mosasaur. Mosasaurs aren't fussy eaters – they will attack anything they can.

million years ago

The Eocene

The Eocene saw some of the earliest whales to move into open water. Among them was basilosaurus, a huge serpentine whale with teeth designed to dismember prey. This whale is a lot less friendly, and considerably more dangerous, than the gummy filter-feeders of the twenty-first century.

The leviathan

The monster sleeps. It's dawn, but there's a furious storm on the horizon and the rising sun is battling to be seen. Purple thunderheads reflected in the sea's surface make it look like a gigantic scarf of maroon silk billowing in the wind. Every so often the monster's sinuous back breaks through. It's swimming slowly, part of its brain still alert to the need to keep moving, to rise to the surface to breathe.

The horizon flickers with lightning and the monster awakes. For a second its head rises out of the water, revealing a long snout etched with deep scars, the result of violent fights with others of its kind, evidence that this is a male. The monster is a whale, but an ancient one – basilosaurus, the most fearsome cetacean ever, on its way to a bloody massacre.

To journey with basilosaurus we've travelled back 36 million years to the Eocene epoch, to a world no longer dominated by giant reptiles. The dinosaurs, pterosaurs and ichthyosaurs are all extinct and their place has been taken by many kinds of mammals. Africa has the early elephant, palaeomastodon, and America the huge hippo-like uintatheres. Asia is home to the brontotheres, giant

Basilosaurus

The first whale to attain a truly gigantic size, it was the largest predator of its day and was equipped with a fairly vicious set of teeth, enabling it to take bigger and more varied prey than later whales.

Name: Means 'regal reptile' or 'king lizard' (although this is inaccurate – see The whale that lost its scales, page 131).
Type of animal: Mammal, an early whale.
When was it alive? 45–36 million years ago (Late Eocene).
Pronunciation: BASS-il-oh-SAWR-uss.
Size: Males 21 metres (70 feet) in length, females 18 metres (60 feet).

Diet: Fish, sharks, squid and small marine mammals.
Fossil finds: North America, Europe, Egypt and New Zealand.
Fact: When scientists first discovered *Basilosaurus* they thought it was the remains of a giant sea serpent.

The Eocene at a glance

How bad? The fourth most dangerous sea of all time.

How long ago? 36 million years.

Where? The Egyptian Sahara Desert just outside Cairo, which at this time is on the coastal fringe of the warm and shallow Tethys Sea.

Shape of the continents: The world's continents are now in roughly the same place as in the twenty-first century. Sea levels are higher, causing marine waters to flood across many of the continents and create inland seas in North Africa, Russia and parts of Europe. Africa is divided from Europe and Asia by the once huge Tethys Sea, which has become little more than a narrow neck of water as the continents have drifted closer together. South America is separate from North America, while the Indian subcontinent is on the verge of impacting into Asia.

What's new? It is 30 million years since the extinction of the dinosaurs and the Earth has seen many changes. The mammals are now the largest animals on the planet and are widespread. The ancestors to all modern mammals, including the whales, hoofed animals, monkeys, apes and carnivores, have evolved. In contrast to the conifers of the dinosaurs' time, flowering plants (angiosperms) dominate the Earth and most of the tree and plant species in the Eocene, including the recently evolved grasses, would be familiar to a modern botanist. The climate is warmer, with a global temperature about 6°C (10°F) higher than today, and a distinct wet and dry season in most places. Rainforests occur over most of the tropics, but further north and south, where it is drier, they give way to more open forests of oak and other deciduous trees. In Antarctica the first polar cap is beginning to form, sending out tongues of cold water into the surrounding oceans.

THE HAZARDS

Top predator: *Basilosaurus.*

Other predators: *Dorudon, Arsinoitherium,* sharks.

On shore: *Arsinoitherium* spends time both in the water and on land – the good news is that it's fairly slow on its feet. Also, 11-metre (36-foot) long *Giganthopis garstini,* the longest snake of all time, ambushes prey from above by waiting in trees before dropping on its victims and crushing the life out of them.

YOU ARE HERE

In the Eocene, mangrove swamps provide a nursery for many fish, including sharks, and food for *Arsinoitherium.*

Two enormous male brontotheres flash their crests during the onset of the mating season. Brontotheres are related to rhinos and horses and are a common feature of the Eocene landscape, browsing in huge herds across much of Asia and America.

rhinoceros-like beasts such as embolotherium, and to massive carnivores such as sarkastodon, which resembles a huge bear. In the seas there are mighty whales such as basilosaurus as well as the smaller species that it hunts.

We're slap bang over the centre of the Sahara Desert, or what will become the Sahara Desert, because for the moment most of North Africa is covered by a shallow continental sea, part of the once-mighty Tethys Sea, an ancient waterway running east–west between Asia and the Atlantic. The nearby coastline is thick with mangrove swamps, backed by dense rainforest filled with a lively cocktail of life: rodents, primitive elephants, hyaenodonts, bats, crocodiles and snakes. Inland lakes and swamps wear a floating cloak of water lilies, and giant lily-trotters tiptoe across the flimsy leaves, their inordinately long toes helping to spread their weight. There is no hint of the great desert that will become this place in the far future.

Just ahead of the whale we're tracking, the water shallows over a sandbank. The basilosaurus doesn't quite run aground, but much of its body is forced above the surface, giving us a better view than we have had so far. Its front limbs are seen to be flippers, with the 'fingers' enclosed in skin, a feature of all whales. Other than that, basilosaurus doesn't look much like a whale at all. Its body is slim and sinuous, some 20 metres (65 feet) long. In fact, it's remarkably similar to the classic description of a lake monster, the one that's allegedly in Loch Ness, for example, or perhaps a sea serpent. The reason for this sleek body is that ancient whales like basilosaurus have none of the blubber that their descendants will develop to keep them warm as they move into colder, even polar waters. Millions of years from now, the blubber of bowhead whales will be more than

The whale that lost its scales

The fossils of the first whales were so snake-like in form that palaeontologists misidentified them as the remains of ancient reptiles. *Basilosaurus*, meaning 'regal lizard' or 'king lizard', was the name bestowed on the first one found in 1832 in Louisiana in the USA. In 1842 the English anatomist Richard Owen correctly identified the animal as a whale and renamed it *Zeuglodon* (meaning 'yoked tooth' because of the double-rooted tooth shape). But the rules of zoological naming culture are strict and the first name a fossil is given has priority. So, however inappropriate, 'king lizard' stuck.

In the second quarter of the nineteenth century, there was another bizarre twist in the story of *Basilosaurus*. An American fossil hunter, Dr Albert C. Koch, collected a large number of ancient whale bones from Alabama and South Carolina. He strung all these bones together, using the vertebrae of at least two animals, and came up with a supposed animal some 34 metres (114 feet) long, which he exhibited as the skeleton of a sea serpent in New York in 1845. He was even cheeky enough to give the creature a scientific name, *Hydrarchos silliman,* very appropriate for such a preposterous reconstruction. (The name was in honour of Professor Benjamin Silliman, a respected scientist who edited the *American Journal of Science and Arts.*) Did Dr Koch's cynical sense of humour lead him to choose this name or was the whole fabrication unintentional and done simply in a fit of enthusiasm? Whatever the truth may be, zoologists were quick to denounce Koch's sea serpent, but the public flocked to see it – fabulous sea monsters, whether real or imagined, were as much of a draw then as they are today.

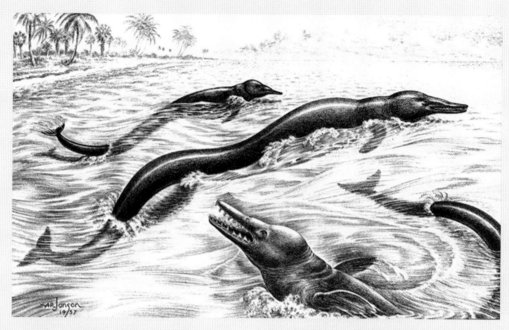

This drawing from the 1950s correctly shows *Basilosaurus* as a whale, but is still influenced by earlier reconstructions of *Basilosaurus* as a sea serpent, with an undulating back.

Important finds were also made in the Fayum Valley in Egypt, 30 kilometres (20 miles) west of Cairo. In the mid-nineteenth century scientists found not only fossilized trees and mangroves, but also hundreds of ancient whale bones eroding out of the desert rocks. The site became an irresistible draw for fossil hunters. In 1907 an expedition was sent from the American Museum of Natural History in New York – the first time American palaeontologists had left their own shores on a fossil hunt. President Theodore Roosevelt himself wrote them a letter of introduction. German and British expeditions followed, but interest in Fayum was short-lived. Then in the 1980s an American professor, Philip Gingerich, one of the world's leading experts on whale fossils, began an extensive study. He and his team excavated 349 skeletons of ancient whales, many of which were baby and adult *Dorudon*, with a few adult *Basilosaurus* scattered among them.

There's irrefutable evidence of the carnivorous nature of *Basilosaurus* – a ball of fish bones has been extracted from the fossilized ribcage of one individual. It contained the remains of several different types of fish, even a shark. The absence of subadult *Dorudon* skeletons led Gingerich to speculate that the area had been a calving ground. He also noticed that some of the baby *Dorudon* had traumatic injuries, crushed skulls, even tooth marks – surely signs of predator attack. *Basilosaurus* is the only predator known from the time powerful enough to inflict this sort of injury, so Gingerich suggested that the 'king lizard' came to the calving ground to hunt the newborn babies.

A blue whale exhales, projecting a 'spout' or 'blow' from its head. In calm conditions experienced whale-watchers may be able to identify a whale just by looking at the shape of its spout. In the Eocene it may have been possible to identify basilosaurus from its spout.

60 centimetres (2 feet) thick. But the early whales of the Tethys have no need for insulation: the brackish waters and shallow seas through which they swim are tepid.

Yet as basilosaurus ploughs over the sandbank, its tail rises up and one glance at that immediately identifies it as a whale. A pair of large flukes held in the horizontal plane causes a tremendous splashing as the tail moves up and down, powering its owner into deeper water. This arrangement of tail flukes and their up-and-down movement are unique to whales and dolphins.

A spout of water vapour, some 4.5 metres (15 feet) high explodes vertically into the air. The basilosaurus is taking a breath with a technique that's another giveaway to its whaleness: it blows stale air out of its lungs and replaces it with fresh. The spout is visible because water droplets form when the relatively warm air expelled from the lungs comes into contact with cooler outside air. To help them take breaths at the surface more easily, the nostrils of future whales will shift back towards the top of the head and become blowholes, with special structures to seal them during a dive.

So, basilosaurus is very much a whale, but other than its snake-like look how does it differ from modern ones? And how is it related to them?

Part of the answer lies at the back of its body, where it has a pair of tiny legs, complete with feet. These are testimony that its ancestors (some 20 million years back) were four-legged land animals, which had begun to move into the water to hunt and feed. From this amphibious way of life some of them made the next step, immersing themselves for their whole lives. There was more than one lineage of these whale-like creatures and it was another line that gave rise to modern whales. Basilosaurus is in fact not an ancestor of modern whales, but an aberrant branch from the common stock of origin.

Hunger pangs

Another difference from modern whales is obvious only when basilosaurus is feeding. The fresh meat it craves is still quite a long way away, so for now it must catch an hors d'oeuvre of seafood. The storm has passed and ethereal creatures shimmer in the sunlit waters ahead. The basilosaurus accelerates into the shoal of squid. As it does so it opens its mouth, revealing a formidable array of teeth. Jerking its head from side to side, it impales its prey, sometimes two squid at a time, on the cone-like teeth at the front of its jaws. Further back inside the mouth, the food is shredded by

A basilosaurus scratches against the sea floor to remove old skin and with it the parasites that plague him – killer whales of the twenty-first century also behave in this way.

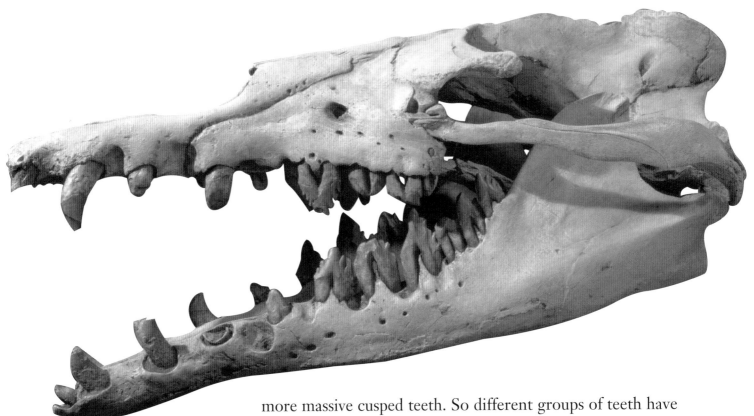

This basilosaurus skull is almost 2 metres (6 feet 6 inches) long and shows the animal's amazing dentition – peg-like teeth at the front for grabbing prey, serrated teeth at the back for slicing through flesh.

more massive cusped teeth. So different groups of teeth have different functions, in contrast to those of modern whales, which have only one kind of conical tooth – if they have any sizeable teeth at all.

The edge taken off its hunger, the basilosaurus continues towards its destination – a gathering of dorudon, another species of ancient whale. It's travelled to these killing fields at the same time of year, the birthing season of its prey, for over a decade. It has a cruising speed of about 10 kilometres (6 miles) an hour; the muscles at the base of its tail are the power-pack that keeps it moving. When the upper muscles contract they bring the tail up, providing the stroke that drives the basilosaurus forward; the lower muscles are half the weight and much less powerful, merely bringing the tail back down in the recovery stroke.

The basilosaurus is in about 6 metres (20 feet) of water, close to a slope of silt rising up to a mangrove swamp. It can hear well underwater and there's a kerfuffle just ahead. It dives to investigate,

Into the ocean

Some 65 million years ago, the mass extinction that killed the dinosaurs also wiped out giant marine reptiles such as the mosasaurs and elasmosaurs, leaving the oceans devoid of any large air-breathing animals. But nature abhors a vacuum and within 10 million years of the dinosaurs' extinction the first mammals were beginning to adapt themselves to life in the water. These were the ancestors of the whales.

The earliest fossils have been found in the Punjab region of Pakistan, in rocks around 55 million years old. Surprisingly, the oldest whales didn't look anything like *Basilosaurus* or modern whales. They had four legs, ears and a tail and resembled wolves. These were the mesonychians, a group of carnivorous mammals that scavenged for stranded fish and drowned animals on the beaches of ancient Pakistan.

The teeth and ear bones of the mesonychians are very similar to those of

Ambulocetus could be described as the missing link between whales and their land ancestors. It lived in river mouths, snatching prey from the water's edge.

The changing shape of whales over the 30 million years it took them to evolve from land predators to ocean-going behemoths. The earliest whales were small and stayed near the coast; later they could travel into open sea, which enabled them to get much bigger.

Basilosaurus and other whales, which is how we can tell that they are related. Other fossils from Pakistan have helped palaeontologists to fill in the 20-million-year gap. We can now see that the whales evolved from four-legged land animals to fully marine creatures by gradually adapting to life in the water. For example, *Ambulocetus* (whose name means 'walking whale') lived in Pakistan around 50 million years ago. With a low, flat body and powerful swimming legs (it resembled a crocodile), it spent its life hunting in rivers and estuaries and probably came ashore only occasionally to rest or sunbathe.

Over time the whales' bodies became more streamlined and their front legs more flipper-like, while their tails flattened out to form powerful swimming flukes. By about 45 million years ago whales were fully adapted to life at sea. The only remaining link with their land ancestry was the pair of tiny vestigial back legs, now used only for guidance during mating.

Most of the early whales were only a few metres in length. *Basilosaurus* was the first of the giants, reaching a length of

20 metres (65 feet). Even though it is instantly recognizable as a whale, it is not directly related to any modern species.

The extinction event at the end of the Eocene saw the demise of *Basilosaurus* and *Dorudon*; shortly after this, around 35 million years ago, the first ancestors to the modern whales appeared. Modern whales can be divided into two main groups: the mysticetes or baleen whales (the blue whale and all the other filter-feeding species) and the odontocetes or toothed whales (the killer whales and dolphins). Both groups quickly adapted to life in the oceans and grew in size and intelligence to become the most common and widespread marine mammal of modern times.

There is one final chapter in the whales' fossil history. Scientists had long suspected that the mesonychian mammals from which the whales evolved were related to modern hoofed animals, meaning that the closest living relatives to the whales would be land animals such as the horse and cow. Sure enough, a recent DNA survey has revealed that the closest genetic relative to the whales is in fact the hippopotamus!

skimming along the muddy bottom. Above it are two shapes the size of rhinos, vigorous strokes of their front legs propelling them through the water. For the basilosaurus this is a chance of a more substantial meal than squid. It accelerates towards the creatures, but they're nearly at the mangrove edge in water too shallow for the hunter to pursue them. Unaware of their narrow escape, one of them turns just in time to see a tail fluke disappear beneath the water as the basilosaurus dives down to continue its voyage.

The creatures are a pair of arsinoitherium, mammals that are in fact distantly related to elephants. Semi-aquatic, the male slightly larger than his mate, they move clumsily on land, their bandy legs giving them a waddling gait. Each has a pair of horns on its head; his are longer and flare out to the side, hers are daintier and upright. They push through the mangroves to a fruiting tree and lasso any fruits within reach with their long and prehensile upper lips.

Arsinoitherium

A huge mammal with distinctive double horns it spent most of its time in the water, but could also come out on land to gorge on vegetation and fruit. It lived like a hippo, looked like a rhino, but was more closely related to the elephant.

Name: Means 'Queen Arsinoe's beast' (Queen Arsinoe ruled Egypt around 300BC).

Type of animal: Mammal, a very distant cousin of the elephant.

When was it alive? 36–30 million years ago, (Late Eocene to Early Oligocene).

Pronunciation: Aars-in-oh-ith-EAR-ee-um.

Size: 1.8 metres (6 feet) high at the shoulder.

Diet: Large fruit and leaves.

Fossil finds: Egypt, Oman, Libya and Angola.

Fact: The giant horns were hollow and may have been used to help it make a bellowing mating call – the position of the horns meant that *Arsinoitherium* was unable to see straight in front of it.

In for the kill

By now the basilosaurus is in the next bay. It has made this trip many times before, so it navigates by hugging the shore, using remembered coastal features, sand spits, rocky promontories, river mouths and the like. When there are no obvious landmarks it finds its way by using the Earth's magnetic field. Now that it's getting close to the end of its journey it is guided by sound, zeroing in on the calls of the dorudon whales it has come here to hunt.

The contact calls between the dorudon grow louder. The basilosaurus heads into the murky waters of a river estuary. It has reached its destination – the dorudon birthing grounds. Clouds of

The position of the male arsinoitherium's horns means that it can only see what's in front of it by cocking its head.

Dorudon

Another species of ancient whale, similar in shape to *Basilosaurus* but a lot smaller. Unlike *Basilosaurus*, it was sociable, spending much of its time in groups. However, *Dorudon* had a much smaller brain than later cetaceans such as dolphins; social interaction between individuals would have been far less sophisticated.

Name: Means 'spear-toothed'.

Type of animal: Mammal, an early whale.

When was it alive? 45–36 million years ago (Late Eocene).

Pronunciation: DOR-oh-don.

Size: 5 metres (16 feet) in length.

Diet: Fish, squid and other swimming animals.

Fossil finds: North America and Egypt.

Fact: With its streamlined body and powerful tail, *Dorudon* was probably the fastest-swimming animal in the Eocene seas.

sediment mean that for much of the time it can see only as far as the tip of its snout – it must rely on sound to pinpoint its prey.

To its left it picks up a loud cry and swirl of mud. Using its front flippers it manoeuvres quickly, shallower strokes of its tail gaining it speed. Now there's a whole cacophony of dorudon calls, both adult and babies. One collides with the basilosaurus' tail as it flees.

A curtain of sediment drops away, so there's a window of visibility. Through it the basilosaurus can make out a small pod of dorudon arranged in a defensive circle, their tails pointing out towards the predator. They're much smaller than it is, only some 4.5 metres (15 feet) or so long. Their grey bodies are tightly packed together, but there's a glimpse of young calves in the centre. Dorudon aren't serpentine in shape and have much more orthodox whale-like proportions than basilosaurus, although they also have limbs at the back as well as flippers at the front.

A subadult dorudon panics, breaking away from the circle. There's a gap in the wall of bodies and the basilosaurus surges through it, seizing a baby dorudon by the head and thrashing it from side to side. The other dorudons scatter, except for the calf's mother, who makes a desultory lunge at the predator. She knows she's too late. Her baby is already dead; the violent shaking has caved in its skull.

Sound in an underwater world

Sound travels much faster and further in water. If we shout at the top of our voice we can be heard about 800 metres (½ mile) away; if a whale 'shouts' in a deep ocean channel, it can be heard 80 kilometres (50 miles) away, so hearing is the whales' most important sense.

As soon as the terrestrial ancestors of whales entered the sea, they had to crack the serious problem of hearing in a watery world. On land, sound waves moving through air are pulled up by the eardrum, so if there's a noise to the left, the sound waves reach the left eardrum first and then travel over the head to the right eardrum. The brain detects the delay between the sound reaching the left and the right ear, so we know the sound is coming from the left. In a similar situation underwater a sound from the left would still hit the left ear first, but would then take a short cut to the right ear by travelling through the skull. The sound information from each ear would arrive at the brain almost instantaneously, making it difficult to calculate the direction it came from – disastrous for predators trying to locate prey or for prey trying to avoid being eaten.

To cope with this problem, whales' ears are separated from the skull and float in a region of fat. Incoming sounds travel through the lower jawbone, which is hollow and packed with fat. Once sound reaches the back of the jaw it is carried to the middle and inner ears via a thin connection of S-shaped bone unique to whales. In the 1980s a series of remarkable discoveries of early whales in Pakistan appeared to suggest that the modern whale ear was already in place over 50 million years ago. *Pakicetus* and *Ambulocetus* already had the S-shaped ear bone and jaws that would have been packed with sound-conducting fat and yet they were still essentially land-based animals. This implies that whale hearing evolved initially not to enable its owner to hear underwater, but for some other purpose. The best guess at the moment is that the animal rested its jawbone on the ground to hear vibrations travelling through the ground rather than through the air. When whales became fully aquatic, the hearing mechanism grew more finely tuned to underwater acoustics. It was pretty well refined by the time of *Basilosaurus* and *Dorudon*.

Like most cetaceans sperm whales use sound to visualize their surroundings. The variety of clicks they emit sounds like hammering to the human ear.

How scary was Basilosaurus?

In the twenty-first-century oceans the sperm whale and the orca or killer whale (technically the largest member of the dolphin family) are the two greatest predatory species. In terms of length, sperm whales are equal to *Basilosaurus*, but killer whales grow to only 9 metres (30 feet), just half the length of the largest *Basilosaurus* and sperm whales.

How about the weaponry for hunting? Sperm whales have 16–30 massive conical teeth in their lower jaws. At 20 centimetres (8 inches) long, they're the largest teeth in the world. Killer whales have 10–14 pairs of large, pointed teeth in the lower and upper jaws. We know that *Basilosaurus* had 40 or so teeth, some for seizing and some for slicing prey. So all three have extremely effective bites.

So far they all seem pretty frightening, but what about the prey they'll tackle? A giant squid, some 12 metres (40 feet) long and weighing 200 kilograms (440 pounds), has been found inside the stomach of a sperm whale. Large and medium-sized squid caught on the seabed are the mainstay of their diet, but they also consume large fish and sharks. As they've never been known to attack or eat mammals, we have no need to fear them. Most of the time they're gentle and benign, although they occasionally used to sink old whaling boats when they were fighting for their life on the end of a harpoon.

Pods of killer whales are adapted to live off the resources provided by the territory they live in. Scientists recognize two main groups: residents, which feed mainly on salmon, tuna or herring, and transients, which feed mainly on mammals, patrolling the haul-outs of seals and sea lions or following large migratory grey or humpback whales. The remains of 24 seals have been found in the stomach of one transient, 13 porpoises and 14 seals in another. However, other than captive orcas not knowing their own strength and killing their keepers, there are no authenticated records of them causing a human death, even though they feed on mammals and a person swimming would be easy prey. The reason for its clean record as far as humans are concerned is probably its large brain. It is thought that killer whales are attracted to potential prey by hearing it move through the water, and are clever enough to realize when they hear humans swimming that they're not a typical food. They may

Orcas or killer whales, famous for their attacks on sea lions off Patagonia, leap out of the water to get their prey within reach of their jaws.

be curious, but perhaps because humans are blubber-free and nutritionally poor, or because they find the strange shape of humans intimidating, they don't attack.

Basilosaurus would probably have been very dangerous to people because its relative brain size was much less than the killer whale's. Like a crocodile, it would see anything swimming in the water as a potential meal and that would bring out its killer instincts. Anything it could overpower would be worth tackling, including humans.

Blood in the water has drawn in two or three physogaleus sharks, so the basilosaurus drags its prey on to a sandbank out of their reach. Water laps around the corpse: it's so shallow here, the predator's head is clear of the sea when it feeds. Lunging at the carcass, the basilosaurus forces open the calf's mouth with its long snout, and bites out its tongue. The monster raises its blood-smeared head and, with one gulp, swallows its prize whole. The basilosaurus' array of formidable and now crimson teeth glistens in the sunlight. It blinks its beady eyes and lowers its head once more to slice off another chunk of meat. Gulping down the bloody flesh it looks truly monstrous, surely the most terrifying whale of all time.

Life really is too short for this dorudon calf. It has become separated from its mother when only a few days old and now has no hope of escaping the jaws of this basilosaurus. Such attacks on dorudon young are an annual occurence.

4

million years ago

The Pliocene

There are sharks and then there is megalodon. This mind-bogglingly large killer fish is 20 times the weight of a great white shark, has teeth the size of a man's hand and preys on full-sized whales by biting their tails off. We should be very relieved that it's now extinct.

Giant sharks

A 3-metre (10-foot) tail fin in the shape of a sabre breaks through the surface of the sea. A shark the length and bulk of a single-decker bus is swimming straight towards you. It seems to be smirking with a mouth over 1 metre (3 feet) across. Working out how bad this situation is depends on what period of history you are in. If you're in the twenty-first century you have no need to worry. The only shark of that size around these days is the whale shark and although its maw is easily capacious enough for you to fit inside, the approaching leviathan won't harm you – it's a creature to marvel at, not flee from; a gentle giant that sustains its huge bulk by filtering tiny planktonic organisms (mullet-sized fish are the largest food it will take) from sea water. Whale sharks do have teeth, several thousand of them arranged in about a dozen rows, but they're tiny and fragile.

However, if you've gone back 4 million years to dive in the Pliocene, things are looking very bad indeed. Here you have just come face to face with a shark that combines great size with almost insatiable flesh-eating tendencies. Megalodon is as colossal as a whale shark, as ferocious as a great white and much more terrifying.

Megalodon

Megalodon was, quite simply, the largest and most dangerous shark of all time. It dwarfed its living relative, the great white shark, and attacked and fed on whales.

Name: Means 'giant teeth'.
Type of animal: A giant shark closely related to living great whites.
When was it alive? 16–1.6 million years ago (Miocene and Pliocene).
Pronunciation: Meg-a-la-don.
Size: 16 metres (52 feet) in length.
Diet: Large fish, dolphins, whales and other large prey.
Fossil finds: Europe, Africa, North and South America, southern Asia, Indonesia, Australia, New Caledonia and New Zealand.
Fact: This giant had a mouth that could open to a width of nearly 3 metres (10 feet). Some people think that *Megalodon* could still be alive today. We hope they're wrong.

A forest of bull kelp, combed by the current. Kelp thrives in colder water and with the world on the brink of an ice age, there will soon be a lot more of it.

YOU ARE HERE

The Pliocene at a glance

How bad? The third most dangerous sea of all time.

How long ago? 4 million years.

Where? Southern Peru, next to the cold oceanic currents flowing north from Antarctica.

Shape of the continents: The shape and pattern of the continents are virtually indistinguishable from those of the modern world. South America is separated from North America by a thin channel of sea. North America and Asia are periodically joined by a land bridge across the Aleutian Islands. Much of the northern and southern polar regions is now obscured by thick ice, but not to the same extent as it will be in the twenty-first century.

What's new? The climate is cooling considerably and is much drier – the Earth is entering the early stages of an ice age. The North and South Poles are dominated by gigantic ice-caps that expand and contract. Mammals dominate both land and sea and live in every conceivable habitat, from the frozen pine forests in the north to the warm rainforests and seas around the Equator. Some show signs of adapting to the colder weather – whales have evolved thick layers of insulating blubber, while mammoths are showing the first signs of a thick covering of hair. The temperate and tropical forests have been replaced by grasslands, home to many new species of mammal – horses, cows and antelopes all roam the plains, while their predators, large cats and dogs, hunt them. In East Africa the hominids are taking the first upright steps on a journey that will end in the evolution of human civilization.

THE HAZARDS

Top predator: *Megalodon*, a close relative of the great white shark, but almost 20 times the size – the largest flesh-eating shark of all time and a specialist killer of whales.

Other predators: Great white shark.

On shore: Large cats and dogs; *Thylacosmilus*, a sabre-toothed marsupial.

Starting small

One of the best places to go looking for megalodon is off the coast of southern Peru. The landscape doesn't look much different from how it will in the twenty-first century, with an arid desert running right to the edge of the coast. But off-shore the rich, fertile waters are teeming with marine life.

You don't want to jump in at the deep end and meet an adult megalodon straight off. Better to familiarize yourself with some juveniles first. Being much smaller than the adults, they go for much smaller prey and so are found in totally separate habitats. To locate a juvenile megalodon you dive close to shore, near colonies of marine mammals, which are like self-service restaurants for flesh-eating sharks. The first step is to decide which prey to choose for your stake-out. Familiar animals such as seals are here, but there are also other, much weirder candidates paddling through the sea – thalassocnus, an aquatic sloth, for one.

Living on the shore, these creatures are caught between the desert and the deep blue sea. There's precious little to eat on the land, so the sloths, which are about the size of grizzly bears, paddle out into the ocean to feed on sea grasses and seaweeds. Their strong back legs are adapted to kick powerfully when swimming and once they're over the aquatic meadows they upend like a duck. Head down, they grab mouthfuls of vegetation, maintaining position by waggling their hairy tails. Sticking around the weeds in the shallows helps protect them from shark attack: megalodon are wary in less than 2 metres (6 feet 6 inches) of water and avoid the cloying feel of weed beds.

A better choice of prey for a megalodon stake-out might be the equally weird odobenocetops leptodon, whose name is a mixture of Greek and Latin meaning 'the whale which seems to walk on its

Fossilized teeth

Sharks usually have one or two rows (some have up to eight) of functional teeth to give them their toothy smile. There isn't much time for the teeth to lose their cutting edge: they're in the front line for only a few days or a week, then their nutrient supply is cut off, the gum tissue holding them dies and they fall out. In their lifetime some sharks lose as many as 20,000 teeth.

Replacements are produced continuously on a conveyor belt of gum tissue on the inside surface of the upper and lower jaws. New teeth are always forming towards the rear of the mouth. Initially angled back, they gradually flip forwards as they move towards the front.

Sharks have been around for over 400 million years, so a mind-boggling number of fallen teeth have ended up on the seabed. Dense and tough, made of calcium phosphate, they fossilize well. *Megalodon* was found in most tropical seas and its fossilized teeth have been found in Europe, Africa, North and South

A brave soul looking for *Megalodon* teeth in the Cooper River, South Carolina. The palaeontological significance of this riverbed wasn't realized until the early 1970s.

America, southern Asia, Indonesia, Australia, New Caledonia and New Zealand. Really big teeth, presumably belonging to really large *Megalodon,* are frequently found in deposits dating back some 3 million years in a site called Sud-Sacaco, south-west of Lima in Peru.

For fossil hunters, the giant teeth of *Megalodon* are particularly precious. If you want to look for them yourself, try Holland, Belgium and England. Head for the public beaches near Zeeuws-Vlaanderen in Holland, or the English beaches of Solent-on-Sea and the Isle of Wight. Florida has many sites – one of the best is Apollo Beach, south of Tampa. Try at low tides and particularly after a storm. Fossils including *Megalodon* teeth are washed onto the shore by

the surf at Jacksonville Beach, east of Jacksonville.

If you're a brave diver, there are exciting opportunities in Cooper River, South Carolina. Currents constantly scour away sand, mud and gravel, uncovering fossil teeth, but you never know how long they'll be revealed before the river engulfs them with sediment. You'd need to hire a professional fossil dive guide – the river currents can be dangerous and visibility is rarely greater than 1.5 metres (5 feet). Sometimes it's so atrocious you can't see your tank pressure gauge, compass, computer or depth gauge. To find your prize, perhaps a 15-centimetre (6-inch) long tooth, you have to grope about blindly on the muddy bottom. Good luck!

Big tooth, little tooth. A fossilized *Megalodon* tooth sits next to one from an Australian great white shark.

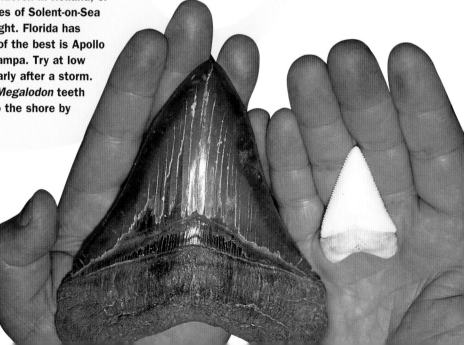

What's in a name?

Ever since the Swedish naturalist Carl Linnaeus devised the zoological system for classifying organisms, names have been all-important to scientists.

Every known species of animal and plant has a two-word scientific name – *Carcharodon carcharias* for the great white shark, for example.

The first name is that of the genus, a group name shared with other, closely related sharks. As it happens there are no contemporary sharks thought to be near cousins of the great white, so it's the only member of the *Carcharodon* genus. As there's usually more than one organism in a genus, the second word, known as the specific name, gives scientists a precise handle to what species they're dealing with.

In the *Sea Monsters* television series and this book, we've called *Megalodon* by its specific name to dodge a controversial issue. There's a major rift between researchers as to whether it should be in the genus *Carcharodon* with the great white or have another generic name, *Carcharocles*. From the 1800s to 1960 it was classified as *Carcharodon megalodon*, then the name was changed to *Carcharocles megalodon*. Today both are contentious.

The pro-*Carcharodon* camp suggests that the great white and *Megalodon* have enough features in common – serrated teeth, for example – to place them in the same genus. These people believe that both creatures evolved from the *Cretolamna* of the early Cenozoic. Pro-*Carcharocles* researchers do not accept that the two mega-carnivores are affiliated and think *Megalodon* arose from an ancient shark called *Otodus obliquus*, in the same group as sand tigers.

The balance seems to be tipping in favour of the *Carcharodon* model (i.e. the belief that *Megalodon* and great white sharks are closely related), but the evidence is ambiguous; palaeontologists need to find the remains of a few more ancient sharks and fill in the gaps in the fossil record before they can fully resolve the mystery.

A breaching great white shark off Seal Island, South Africa. Great whites use deep water to accelerate up to the surface to attack Cape fur seals.

teeth'. It lives by snaffling up food from the bottom mud, so you need to dive to join it, seeking the security of a kelp forest on the seabed. Megalodon shouldn't attack you amongst the fronds and by remaining hidden you can avoid disturbing their potential prey.

Although they're related to modern monodontid whales such as the beluga and narwhal, odobenocetops look like a cross between a walrus and a manatee. In size and shape they are reminiscent of manatees, some 2 metres (6 feet 6 inches) long – manatees can grow to 4 metres (13 feet) – with torpedo-shaped bodies, V-shaped tails and paddle-like forelimbs which they use to manoeuvre, by pivoting, sculling or paddling. They feed like walruses, using highly sensitive whiskers on their upper lip and cheeks to find and identify food in the seafloor sediment. Producing suction with their well-developed cheeks, they hoover up crustaceans and molluscs. When they are successful, you can see puffs of mud and hear slurping sounds.

Another characteristic odobenocetops share with walruses is a pair of tusks sweeping back from their rubbery lips. In this respect males are different from females. Females have two tusks of the same size, about 25 centimetres (10 inches) long. The male's left tusk is a similar length, but the right one can reach an extraordinary 1.35 metres (4 feet 6 inches) and is presumably used in battles with other males during the breeding season. Many male odobenocetops have scars and wounds on their heads, even broken tusks, which tend to indicate that they fight amongst themselves.

Enthralled by these beguiling creatures, you could easily forget what this dive is for, but then a shape skims past the edge of the kelp towards you. It is a megalodon, some 3 metres (10 feet) long and with a much heavier build that a great white shark of the same size. Tornadoes of silt swirl away from the beating tails of the odobenocetops feeding in the open as they seek cover in the kelp beds. The shark passes over your head, so close that you could stretch up and touch it. There is a narrow slit about 30 centimetres

Odobenocetops
are a favourite prey of
megalodon. Dense beds of
kelp offer some protection,
as the predators are
wary of penetrating
the fronds.

(1 foot) long in the middle of its belly, an umbilical scar showing where it was attached to its mother (many sharks give birth to living young, nourished during their earliest development through a placenta-like attachment to the female). Only very young sharks show this slit; it disappears when they're a few months old, so this not-so-small creature is a pup. If the babies are as big as that, imagine what the mother is going to be like ….

The patrolling predator keeps close to the kelp so that dappled light on its steel-grey back helps it to disappear into the background of swaying fronds. Sooner or later an odobenocetops will surface to breathe and then the megalodon will strike from below, rushing upwards at speeds of more than 60 kilometres (40 miles) an hour. These attacks can be so cataclysmic that the sharks shoot into the air like rockets, sometimes with prey clamped between their teeth.

Ambushing prey like this gives the shark a chance to deliver a devastating bite before backing off. It then waits until the prey is weakened from blood loss before following up with the *coup de grâce*. Such behaviour minimizes the risk of injury when fighting with large prey; the megalodon has delicate eyes and can't afford to have them scratched by the tusk of a struggling odobenocetops.

You still have to meet an adult, and the most reliable way to do that is to track their favourite prey. After spending their early years perfecting their 'maim first, kill later' hunting strategy on seals, odobenocetops and porpoises, full-grown megalodon graduate to become killers of whales out in the open ocean. So you are very unlikely to see an adult among these shallow kelp beds. Careful not to look like a tasty odobenocetops going up for air, you climb straight up a large kelp plant, pulling yourself up arm over arm. Once safely back on board your boat, you can head out into deeper water where it gets *really* dangerous.

Odobenocetops

A strange-looking type of extinct whale that lived off the coast of Peru where it grubbed in the mud with its mouth, looking for food. Its most notable features were the male's tusks, one of which (always on the animal's right) could reach 1.35 metres (4 feet 6 inches).

Name: Means 'the whale which seems to walk on its teeth', because of its long tusks.

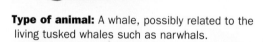

Type of animal: A whale, possibly related to the living tusked whales such as narwhals.

When was it alive? Around 3–5 million years ago (Pliocene).

Pronunciation: Ode-oh-ben-oh-sey-tops.

Size: 2.1 metres (7 feet) in length.

Diet: Clams, worms and other mud-dwelling animals.

Fossil finds: Peru.

Fact: The males used their long tusks to joust with each other during the mating season.

Swimming with sharks

Although *Megalodon* was the biggest and the most dangerous shark ever, in the twenty-first century the 'biggest' and the 'most dangerous' sharks are two completely separate species: the whale shark and the great white. As a zoologist I (Nigel Marven) have encountered both and the two experiences couldn't have been more different.

The ocean side of Ningaloo reef in Western Australia is one of the best places in the world to catch up with whale sharks. As one swam beneath me I could see the patterns of white lines and a mosaic of white polka dots on its blue-grey skin. This 'dot and dash' arrangement is as unique as a human fingerprint and the markings can be used to identify individual whale sharks.

The shark disappeared into the deep. It was about 6 metres (20 feet) long and probably weighed 6 tonnes. Whale sharks are the largest fish alive today – individuals between 10 and 12 metres (33 and 40 feet) are not uncommon. It's claimed that one caught at Baba Island, near Karachi, Pakistan, in 1949 measured 20 metres (65 feet) in length, was 7 metres (23 feet) around the thickest part of its body and weighed 20 tonnes.

The biggest flesh-eating shark is the great white. There are plenty of fisherman's tales about their size, but adults average 4.3–4.6 metres (14–15 feet) in length, with a weight of 322–770 kilograms (710–1700 pounds). The largest authenticated specimen, caught by Alfred Cutajar off the coast of Malta in 1987, was 7.6 metres (25 feet) long.

Free swimming with a great white is an entirely different proposition from swimming with a whale shark. The conditions must be perfect, the sea mustn't be too choppy and you need underwater visibility of 10 metres (33 feet) or so. You have to be able to keep an eye on the shark and, most importantly, it needs to see you clearly. If there's clarity, it will probably recognize that you're not a blubbery seal or sea lion. In murky water it might attack on the off chance that you are edible.

I've been lucky enough to swim in open water with great whites near the small town of Gansbaai, near the tip of South Africa. I'll never forget the first time I slipped into the water, knowing that a great white was circling our boat. When I nervously put my head beneath the surface, the shark was just 10 metres (33 feet) away. It was a female – I could tell by the absence of claspers. The rush of adrenaline made me gulp a huge breath of air through my snorkel tube. The shark's partially open mouth gave her a smile like a clown and also meant that whenever I looked at her, those triangular teeth were always on show.

I felt I was watching a jet fighter, not a mere fish. She moved effortlessly with languid sweeps of her tail. Braking and precise turns were done by flexing her pectoral fins, which flared out like wings just behind her head. I hadn't noticed, but the distance between her and me had been halved. She hovered in the water – maybe she was curious about this strange, pink-masked apparition. She was about 5 metres (16 feet) long, an imposing length, but it was her girth that impressed me most. With most giant creatures a small increase in length brings on a disproportionate hike in bulk. If I'd wanted to cuddle her, my arms wouldn't have been long enough to encircle her body.

Even so, she would have been dwarfed by that whale shark in Western Australia. That's a harmless plankton eater, but because of its sheer size my heart had been in my mouth. With the great white my heart went into my mouth, too, and it stopped for a moment. That effect on my 'ticker' was due to her potential as a predator. If this creature wanted to, she could slice me in two with a single bite.

If you free swim with a great white shark you might need a short metal stick or uncocked harpoon to rap it on the nose if it gets too inquisitive.

The whale killer

Originating near Antarctica, a cold, nutrient-laden ocean current creeps along the seafloor until it collides with the edge of the South American continent. Here, off the Peruvian coast, it wells upwards, bringing with it a bounty of marine life. The increase in nutrients allows floating microscopic plants to thrive; they are fed upon by tiny planktonic animals, the larvae of fish, crustaceans and jellyfish. These in turn provide a feast for larger larvae of fish, crustaceans and jellyfish.

This planktonic soup is rich enough to sustain the massive bodies of baleen whales, and you soon happen across a school of them. They feed by gulping in mouthfuls of water, which are then forced out through a series of plates growing down from each side of the upper jaw. Along these plates are bristles that act like sieves in which the planktonic flotsam is trapped. The whale uses its huge tongue to wipe the food from these fringes and then swallows it. These particular whales are a species that is not familiar in the twenty-first century, but they're similar to Bryde's whale, a mid-size kind, up to 15 metres (50 feet) long, with a dark grey upper body, lighter grey below. With any luck a megalodon will follow the whales, so from the boat you scan the ocean for any tell-tale sign.

The chances of actually seeing a kill are slim, but a cloud of swirling gulls leads you to what is probably the aftermath of one. The corpse of a whale rocks gently in the swell, but the serenity of the motion belies the ferocity of the scene. The water is red with blood and there are gaping holes edged with tattered flesh in the whale's throat. The screaming gulls wheel above, every so often diving down to pick off gobbets of congealed blood or titbits of meat.

Every 30 seconds or so the whole corpse shivers as a shark takes a bite from it. You count at least a dozen triangular dorsal fins, some

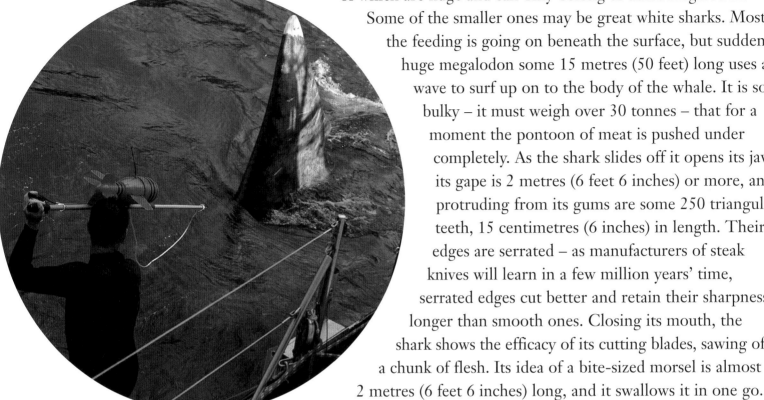

Nigel attaches a camera to the back of a passing megalodon to get a shark's-eye view of the underwater world.

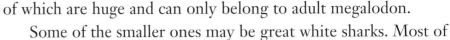

of which are huge and can only belong to adult megalodon. Some of the smaller ones may be great white sharks. Most of the feeding is going on beneath the surface, but suddenly a huge megalodon some 15 metres (50 feet) long uses a wave to surf up on to the body of the whale. It is so bulky – it must weigh over 30 tonnes – that for a moment the pontoon of meat is pushed under completely. As the shark slides off it opens its jaws – its gape is 2 metres (6 feet 6 inches) or more, and protruding from its gums are some 250 triangular teeth, 15 centimetres (6 inches) in length. Their edges are serrated – as manufacturers of steak knives will learn in a few million years' time, serrated edges cut better and retain their sharpness longer than smooth ones. Closing its mouth, the shark shows the efficacy of its cutting blades, sawing off a chunk of flesh. Its idea of a bite-sized morsel is almost 2 metres (6 feet 6 inches) long, and it swallows it in one go.

At first it's difficult to tell if the megalodon and other sharks are scavenging on a whale that has died of natural causes or whether one of them has hunted it down. The corpse's flippers have hideous bite marks and as this is not a very succulent part of the whale, it's likely the feeding sharks would leave it until last. The damage may have been inflicted when the whale was still alive, by a megalodon trying to cripple it. As if on cue to endorse this theory, a lunge from a shark pushes the whale's back above the water to reveal that a large part of the tail is missing. So this whale probably was a victim of a megalodon – injured so utterly by the first strike that it could no longer swim to the surface to breathe. It would have died from a combination of blood loss, drowning and further attacks. This once mighty creature has been reduced to nothing more than a feeding station – and your opportunity to come face to face with a megalodon.

From the crow's nest of Nigel's boat it's easy to appreciate the true size of the megalodon passing underneath.

Looking death in the face

Even though the sharks will probably be fully occupied gorging themselves on the whale for a while, in a feeding frenzy like this things can get out of hand, so you need the protection of a shark cage tethered to the boat.

The underwater view is awe-inspiring. There are sharks everywhere. Some of them have bellies bloated from the meat they've gulped down, others have their heads buried in the corpse like pigs at a trough. Just as you thought, there are eight great whites in the mêlée. The three megalodon in view are all subadults two or three times the size of the newborn you met with the odobenocetops. Impressive enough, but where is the adult you saw riding a wave on to the whale's back to rip away a chunk of flesh?

When the other sharks scatter, you know it is somewhere near. As you glance down between your feet the thick metal bars you are

A close up of the teeth of a megalodon, from inside Nigel's shark cage. These triangular weapons are serrated, just like steak knives, to slice through flesh and to keep sharp for longer. Megalodon teeth can be 15 centimetres (6 inches) long.

standing on suddenly look alarmingly flimsy. The megalodon is below you. Its broad back has two dorsal fins, the larger a graceful triangular sail, the smaller one a diamond shape further back, in front of the tail. It has more of a snub nose than a great white, whose snout is so pointy that in Australia it's nicknamed white pointer. Beneath the vast body you can see a pair of claspers trailing in the water behind, revealing that this individual is a male – claspers are sausage-shaped tubes at the base of the tail used for implanting sperm inside the female during mating.

The predator senses something above him. Curious, he does a wide loop, simultaneously rising up in the water column so that when he comes towards you, you are at eye level. He looks straight at you with eyes of black satin; yours nearly pop out of your head. But they still take in every detail of the mega-carnivore heading towards you. The shark isn't just relying on its eyes; it is using other sensory systems of extraordinary sensitivity to investigate the cage with its strange occupant.

A shaft of sunlight dances over its head, illuminating what looks like a five-o'clock shadow around its mouth and chin. This isn't stubble, however; the scattered black dots are the pores of what will come to be known as the ampullae of Lorezini, after the Italian anatomist who first describes them in 1878. These structures enable sharks to detect electrical fields in the water. The pores open out into jelly-filled canals infiltrated by nerves. If there are any objects in the vicinity emanating electricity, impulses are fired to the brain. The megalodon will be sensing your beating heart and the impulses flashing through your muscles when you make any movement.

If you move, as well as producing this body electricity, you'll also create water currents which sharks can detect, too. Now the

With jaws opened fully, the gape of a megalodon measures up to 2.5 metres (8 feet) across. The only safe way to see the jaws is when their owner is long dead.

Dos and don'ts of diving with Megalodon

To give yourself the best chance of seeing *Megalodon* safely, you would need to head back to the Pliocene with a boat big enough to hold a shark cage, breathing apparatus and buckets of foul-smelling fish guts, whale blubber, blood and offal. Also, ask yourself whether your boat could stand up to an attack from a shark the size of a large whale; sharks do attack boats, and in *Megalodon*'s case that could be quite destructive.

Next, you would need to anchor up in some likely habitat, perhaps next to a colony of marine mammals or over an underwater cliff or canyon; these are often patrolled by oceanic sharks such as *Megalodon*. The blood and offal on board are crucial for making a disgusting concoction called 'chum'. Even if the sea sickness hasn't got to you, just one whiff of this liquid is guaranteed to make you feel queasy. Sharks, however, love it and when it's ladled over the side of the boat, it forms a slick in the current and acts as an irresistible 'come hither and eat me' signal. With luck, a *Megalodon* crossing this odour corridor will follow it right to its source.

Once a *Megalodon* have been attracted to the boat, you need to keep it interested. Throw out a large piece of bait on a rope, pulling it out of range just before it's chomped, then throw it again. Now's the time to lower the cage into the water, don your wet suit and carefully get inside. Get somebody on deck to use the bait to entice the shark or sharks in front of you. In the cramped confines of a cage you won't be able to wear a scuba tank – instead, leave the cylinder on deck, run an air hose down into the cage and breathe through that.

After many encounters like this you might decide you have met a placid *Megalodon*. If the visibility is good enough and you have enough people to back you up, you could try free swimming outside the cage, although we're not sure we'd advise it. This is a monster that chomps huge whales, and it might use you as a toothpick.

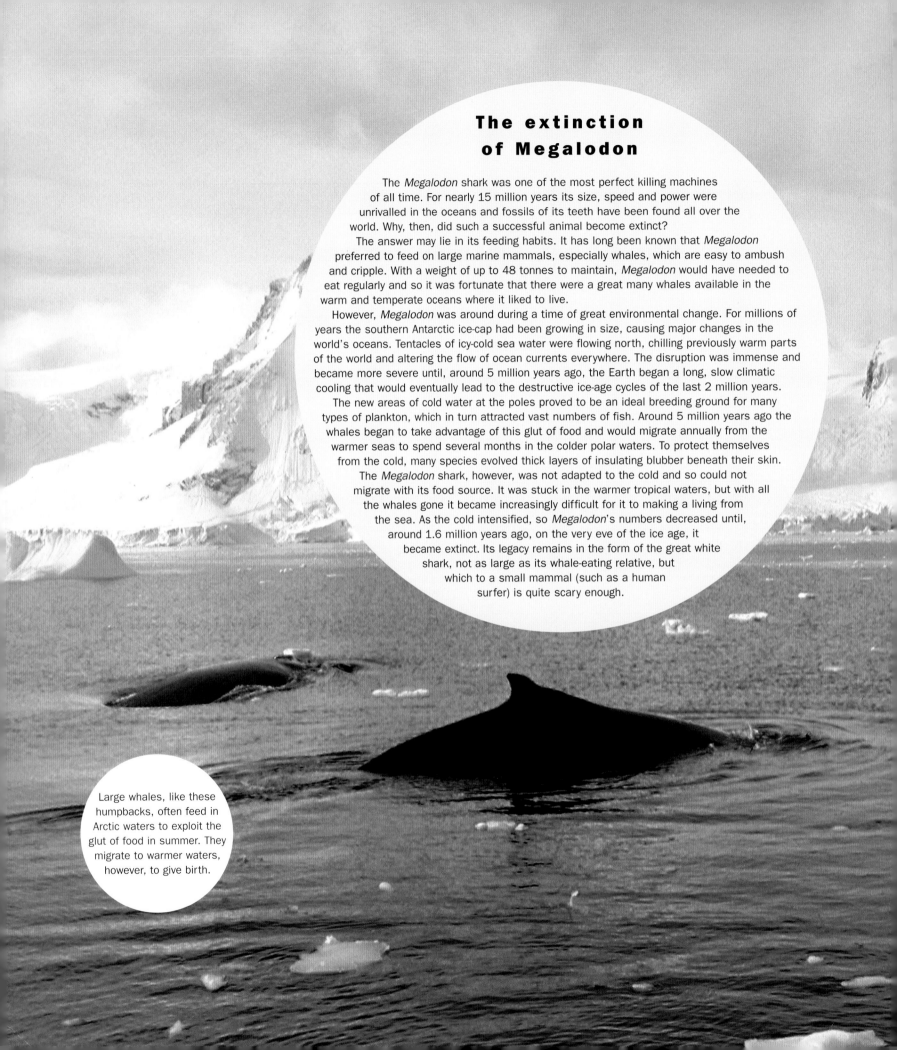

The extinction of Megalodon

The *Megalodon* shark was one of the most perfect killing machines of all time. For nearly 15 million years its size, speed and power were unrivalled in the oceans and fossils of its teeth have been found all over the world. Why, then, did such a successful animal become extinct?

The answer may lie in its feeding habits. It has long been known that *Megalodon* preferred to feed on large marine mammals, especially whales, which are easy to ambush and cripple. With a weight of up to 48 tonnes to maintain, *Megalodon* would have needed to eat regularly and so it was fortunate that there were a great many whales available in the warm and temperate oceans where it liked to live.

However, *Megalodon* was around during a time of great environmental change. For millions of years the southern Antarctic ice-cap had been growing in size, causing major changes in the world's oceans. Tentacles of icy-cold sea water were flowing north, chilling previously warm parts of the world and altering the flow of ocean currents everywhere. The disruption was immense and became more severe until, around 5 million years ago, the Earth began a long, slow climatic cooling that would eventually lead to the destructive ice-age cycles of the last 2 million years.

The new areas of cold water at the poles proved to be an ideal breeding ground for many types of plankton, which in turn attracted vast numbers of fish. Around 5 million years ago the whales began to take advantage of this glut of food and would migrate annually from the warmer seas to spend several months in the colder polar waters. To protect themselves from the cold, many species evolved thick layers of insulating blubber beneath their skin.

The *Megalodon* shark, however, was not adapted to the cold and so could not migrate with its food source. It was stuck in the warmer tropical waters, but with all the whales gone it became increasingly difficult for it to making a living from the sea. As the cold intensified, so *Megalodon*'s numbers decreased until, around 1.6 million years ago, on the very eve of the ice age, it became extinct. Its legacy remains in the form of the great white shark, not as large as its whale-eating relative, but which to a small mammal (such as a human surfer) is quite scary enough.

Large whales, like these humpbacks, often feed in Arctic waters to exploit the glut of food in summer. They migrate to warmer waters, however, to give birth.

megalodon is broadside on, you can see lines of large pores running along the middle of its immense flank and branching out into a tracery around its face called the lateral line system. Each organ on the lateral line contains a lump of jelly and if one of those bends because of perturbations in the water, a message is sent to the brain. It's a bit like humans feeling wind against their cheeks. The megalodon senses the water movement as you scull with your arms to maintain position in the cage.

The monster slows but still keeps coming forward, now only an arm's length away. Instinctively, you back off to the far side of the cage. The metal bars are producing a weak electric field and the megalodon is investigating this phenomenon. Without arms or tentacles, sharks that are curious about an object must use their mouths to check it out. This one opens its mouth wide. You are looking right down the throat of the biggest shark that's ever lived. There's a clunk as the cutting blades that are its teeth hit the iron bars. The sensors in its mouth, jaws and teeth tell it that this isn't an object that can be eaten – it tastes wrong, for a start, and there's no soft tissue or blubber. The megalodon shakes its monstrous head and with one sweep of its mighty tail turns back towards the whale carcass. You, however, aren't going anywhere – your limbs are frozen with fear and it is only the ragged sound of your own breathing that convinces you that you're still alive.

After this experience, any time-travelling diver would be shaken up. Before the encounter there were no guarantees that the metal bars would hold up to a megalodon; the strength needed for the cage could only be calculated from scaling up a great white shark and predicting its power if it grew to be 15 metres (50 feet) long. The cage did withstand the megalodon, however, and the creature that mouthed the bars, the sea monster whose throat you've looked into, didn't spring from the imagination of a Hollywood film producer. This was the biggest flesh-eating shark that's ever lived.

Acknowledgements

Thank you to Tim Haines, the driving force for the revolutionary series, *Walking with Dinosaurs*, who asked me to be the presenter for *Sea Monsters*, to give scale and context to the prehistoric creatures. My co-author, Jasper James, director and series producer of this ambitious series, immersed me in the seven deadliest seas of all time. By reading a myriad scientific papers and picking the brains of the experts who wrote them, Jasper and his team did their utmost to make their computer-generated creatures and the environments they inhabited as authentic as possible. Then I had to act as if the creatures were actually there and acting is something I'd never done before, but I've met alligators in the flesh, so, by scaling them up in my mind's eye to the size of a mosasaur and reacting accordingly, I managed to scrape through this daunting challenge. After that it was down to the camera magic of cinematographer Michael Pitts and the computer wizardry of Framestore CFC. The results of their efforts, as you can see from the series and the images in this book, are staggering. When I'm an old man looking back on it all, I think I may actually believe I dived with real sea monsters.

So I owe a massive debt of gratitude to all the people behind the production of the series and of the book as well. Jasper has listed them below and I would like to join him in thanking them all for their hard work.

I must also thank Fiona Seager for inputting my longhand scrawl and deciphering faxes written on planes and sent from all over the globe. The help of Matthew Wright was also invaluable, with his meticulous checking and finding of facts, often at ungodly hours. And finally thank you to the readers, for reading and watching.

NIGEL MARVEN

If I thanked all the people I wanted to, there'd be a list of about 100 people here, because just about everyone who worked on the TV series contributed either directly or indirectly to the book as well. This, then, is the executive summary: my enormous appreciation goes out to the graphics team at Framestore CFC for making extinct animals real – special thanks to Mike Milne, Max Tyrie and Tim Greenwood. Extra special thanks to Daren Horley who created many of the pictures in this book and to George Roper who designed the time map. Big dollops of gratitude also to Mike Pitts for his underwater stills, Paul Chambers and Alex Freeman for their amazing research on which this book is based, Michael Davis for stills wrangling, the whole team at Impossible Pictures for keeping the show on the road and Crawley Creatures for making the best animatronics ever to be thrown in the sea.

Then there's the team who pulled the book together from the maelstrom of drafts, ever-changing pictures and fossils from obscure museums around the world: hats off and thanks to all those at BBC Books, especially Shirley Patton, Nicky Ross, Sarah Miles, Caroline Taggart, Linda Blakemore, Martin Hendry, Miriam Hyman and Claire Parker.

And, most importantly, thank you to my wonderful wife Amber for doing without her husband for the many evenings and weekends it took to write this, Poppy for doing without her daddy and little Holly for not being born until just after I'd finished the manuscript!

JASPER JAMES

Picture credits

Academy of Natural Sciences, Philadelphia 118 centre; Ardea 26 (David & Katie Urry), 32 top and 54 (Pat Morris), 80 top (John Cancalosi), 89 bottom left and 132 and 139 (Francois Gohier), 113 bottom (Hans & Judy Beste); Cleveland Museum of Natural History 61; Corbis 80 bottom (Galen Rowell); Mike Everhart 75, 110, 113 top, 118 bottom; Geo Science Features Picture Library 89 top centre (Martin Land); Robert Harding 88 top (L Frost), 140; Chad Henning 152; Hulton Getty 10; Institut und Museum fur Geologie und Palaontologie der Universitat Tubingen 101; Mary Evans Picture Library 41 (E Etherington); Patrick McCarthy 147 top (Kevin Rooney); Nature Picture Library 81 top and 89 top right (Jurgen Freund), 147 bottom (Jeff Rotman), 160 (Ben Osborne); Natural History Museum 118 top; 89 NHPA 28 (Alberto Nardi), 35 left and 78 left (Daniel Heuclin), 48 (Ant Photo Library), 55 (Dr Ivan Polunin), 81 bottom (Kevin Schafer); Oxford Scientific Films 15 top (Breck P Kent), 16 (Zig Lesczysnski), 39 (Joe McDonald), 86 (NASA), 89 bottom right (David M Dennis); Peabody Museum of Natural History, Yale University 119 bottom; Science Photo Library 32 bottom and 33 (Sinclair Stammers), 56 (Peter Scoones); Seapics.com 11 (Doug Perrine), 103 (Mark Conlin), 148; Sternberg Museum of Natural History 121 bottom left; University of Michigan Exhibit Museum of Natural History 134.

Production stills by Jasper James 34, 72, 157; Samantha Jukes-Adams 69; Ian MacDonald 154; Michael Pitts 1, 7, 17, 23, 29, 37, 43, 49, 57, 62, 68, 70, 98, 114, 120, 129, 168.

All other pictures, including digital images created by Framestore CFC, are © BBC 2003, apart from the following, which are © BBC Worldwide: 21, 46–7, 66, 71, 83, 87, 88, 90, 92–3, 94, 97, 99, 100, 102, 107, 116–17, 126–7, 130, 133, 135, 138, 141, 142–3.

Index

Page numbers in *italics* refer to illustrations, and those in **bold** refer to creature profile boxes.

Dorudon 21, **138**, *138*
  excavation of skeletons 131
  predation of calves by *Basilosaurus* 131,
    134, 136, 139, 141, *141*
Dromaeosaurus 107
Dunkleosteus 7, 12, 15, *46–7*, 50, **50**, 60,
    61, 62–3
  fossil of *61*
  protection of divers *52–3*
  regurgitation *63*
  teeth 51

ears, of whales 139
Earth, conditions 4 billion years ago 10
egg-laying by nothosaurs 66, 69
eggs, reptiles' *69*
Elasmosaurus 15, 114, *116–17*, **117**, 119
  reconstructions of skeleton 118, *118*
electrical fields, detection by sharks 157,
    161
Embolotherium 130
English countryside, modern and Jurassic
    88
Eocene period 126–41
Euhoplites opalinus 89
Eusthenopteron 55
Eustreptospondylus 87, *87*
eurypterids (sea scorpions) *34*, 34–6, **35**,
    36, *37*
  fossil of *35*
  mating behaviour 36, *38*, 39–40
  moulting 36, 39
evolution
  of birds 110
  parallel 113
  of whales 135
extinction
  of dinosaurs 20, 135
  of *Megalodon* 160
eyesight
  of Ordovician creatures 45
  of trilobites 33
  see also stereoscopic vision

Fayum Valley, Egypt 131
fish
  adaptation to life on land 55
  diversity of species 48

jawless 57–8
  mass extinction 63
'fish within a fish' fossil *121*
Fishes, Age of (Devonian) 46–63
fossils
  of *Dunkleosteus* 61
  living 56
  oldest dinosaur fossil 71
  of sea scorpion 35
  sharks' teeth 147, *147*
  of vomit (palaeolags) 61, *63*

Gastornis 20
gastroliths 119
gharials 74
The Giant Claw 6
giant ichthyosaurs 75
  see also ichthyosaurs
giant mosasaurs 122, **122**, 124, *125*
  see also mosasaurs
giant orthocone (*Cameroceras*) 12, **40**
  see also orthocones
giant sharks 144
  see also Megalodon
giant squid 107, 114
  as prey of sperm whales 140
giant trilobite **31**
  see also trilobites
Giganthopis garstini 129
Giganotosaurus 6, 96
Gingerich, Philip (palaeontologist) 131
Globidens 112
Gondwana 27, 49, 70, 87
graptolites 51, **51**
grass snakes 6
great crested newts 6
great white sharks (*Carcharodon carcharias*)
    148, *148*, 160
  feeding with *Megalodon* 154, 156
  swimming with 152, *152*

Hainosaurus 107, 122, **122**
Halisaurus *111*, 112, **112**
hatchetfish 48
hearing mechanisms
  in *Cryptoclidus* 103
  in whales 139
Herrerasaurus 71

Hesperornis 108–10, *109*, **109**
  predation by *Hainosaurus* 122
  predation by *Halisaurus* 112
hippopotamus, kinship with whales 135
hominids, appearance in Pliocene 145
horse-shoe crabs *39*
humpback whales *160*
hurricane Emilia *86*
Hybodus 88, *94*, 103, **103**
Hydrarchos silliman 131
hyponome of orthocones 42, 44

ice ages 17
  role in extinction of *Megalodon* 160
ice caps, formation 129
ichthyosaurs *8*, 18, 19, 74, 75, 96
  see also Cymbospondylus
Ichthyostega 55
iguana, marine 80, *80*
insects 107
  first appearance 49
  see also arthropods
ironing board shark *see Stethacanthus*
Isotelus **31**

jawless fish *15*
jellyfish 28
jet propulsion of orthocones 42, 44
Jurassic period 19, 84–103

Kansas in Cretaceous period 106, 108
kelp *145*
killer whales (orcas) 133, 140, *140*
Koch, Albert C. 131
komodo dragons 6
kraken *41*

labyrinthodonts 13
lamprey *15*
Land of Giants 6
land life
  emergence of 16, 26, 49, 50
  problems with 28
landfish 16
Latimeria chalumnae 56
  see also coelacanths
Laurasia 70, 87
Laurentia 27, 30, 49, 50

S-shaped ear bone 139
Sahara Desert 130
salt elimination by marine reptiles 69, 80
saltwater crocodile *80*, 80
Sarcosuchus 18
Sarkastodon 130
scrub python *113*
sea level in Jurassic era 86
sea scorpions (eurypterids) 7, 12, 13, *34*, 34–6, **35**, *36*, *37*
    fossil of *35*
    mating behaviour 36, *38*, 39–40
    moulting 36, 39
    vision 45
sea serpent skeleton 131
sea serpents 130
sea snakes 81
sense of smell of *Liopleurodon* 99–100
sexual reproduction in placoderms 61
shark attacks, prevention by smell suits 99
shark cages 53
    for diving with *Megalodon* 161
sharks 7, 13, 16, 20
    Cladoselache 58
    in Cretaceous 112, 114
    dorsal fin spikes 103
    giant 144
    Mexican hornshark *103*
    physogaleus 141
    swimming with 152
    teeth 58, 96, 147, *147*
    whale sharks 91
    see also; great white sharks; *Hybodus*; *Megalodon*; *Stethacanthus*
Shonisaurus 19, 75
sight *see* eyesight; stereoscopic vision
Silliman, Benjamin 131
Silurian period 61
sloth, aquatic (*Thalassocnus*) 146
smell suits 98, 99
snakes 6
    first appearance 107
    Giganthopis garstini 129
    ingestion of prey 113
    kinship with mosasaurs 113
    marine 81

sound, underwater transmission 139
speed
    of *Basilosaurus* 134
    of giant mosasaurs 124
    of *Xiphactinus* 121–2
sperm whales 96, *139*
    comparison with *Basilosaurus* 140
spherical diving cage *62*
Squalicorax 107, 114
Stegosaurus 14
stereoscopic vision 36
    see also eyesight
Stethacanthus (ironing board shark) 13, 16, **58**, *59*, 60
stones, ingestion by plesiosaurs 119
storms in Jurassic era 87
stromatolites *11*
Sud-Sacaco, discovery of *Megalodon* teeth 147
survival techniques 100, 103

tail-shedding (autotomy) *78*, 78–9
Tanystropheus 7, 13, 18, **73**, *73*–4, *78*
    tail-shedding 78–9
Tarbosaurus 6, 6
teeth
    of *Basilosaurus* 133–4
    birds' 110
    of *Leedsichthys* 95
    of *Megalodon* 154, *156*, *157*
    of nothosaurs *70*
    of placodonts 72
    pterygoid 112, 113, *113*
    replacement in mosasaurs 124
    sharks' 58, 96, 147, *147*
Tethys sea 129, 130
Thalassocnus 146
therapods 71
Therizinosaurus 6
Thylacosmilus 145
time line 12–15
toothed birds *see Hesperornis*
toothed whales (odontocetes) 135
transient whales 140
Triassic period 19, 64–83
trilobites 12, *13*, 32–3
    Asaphus kowalewskii 32
    Ceraurinella ingrica 32

defence posture *33*
    giant **31**
    Isotelus **31**
    vision 45
Tulerpeton 55
turtles
    leatherback 80–1, *81*
    see also Archelon
Tylosaurus **122**
Tyrannosaurus rex 15, 71, *107*, **108**

Uintatheres 128

Velociraptor 19
vertebrates 11
vision, stereoscopic 36
    see also eyesight
volcanoes 10, *10*
vomit, fossilized (palaeolags) 61, *63*

Western Interior Seaway *106*
whale sharks 91, 144
    swimming with 152
whales
    baleen whales 153
    blue whales *132*
    evolution of 21–2, 135
    hearing mechanisms 139
    humpback whales *160*
    killer whales (orcas) 133, 140, *140*
    Pakicetus 139
    sperm whales 96
    see also Ambulocetus; *Basilosaurus*; *Dorudon*
woolly mammoth 15, 145

Xiphactinus 14, 19, *104–5*, 107, **121**, 121–2
    skeleton *121*

Zeuglodon 131
    see also Basilosaurus